T-SHIRT WISDOM FOR THE GRADUATE

CLIFF SCHIMMELS

OLIVER NELSON

A Division of Thomas Nelson Publishers
Nashville

Published in Nashville, Tennessee, by Oliver-Nelson Books, a division of Thomas Nelson, Inc., Publishers, and distributed in Canada by Lawson Falle, Ltd., Cambridge,
Ontario.

Unless otherwise noted, the Bible version used in this publication is THE NEW KING
JAMES VERSION. Copyright © 1979, 1980, 1982, Thomas Nelson, Inc., Publishers.

Printed in the United States of America.

ISBN 0-8407-9575-0

1 2 3 4 5 6 — 96 95 94 93 92 91

Contents

Acknowledgments   vii
Introduction   9

1. You Are Here, But Where Am I?   11
2. Transitions Taste Like Spinach   15
3. Quiet: Decision in Progress   19
4. God Loves Spunk   24
5. Cackle When You're Finished   30
6. Catching Fish Is Better Than Chasing Rats   35
7. I'm Not Afraid to Catch What I'm Chasing   39
8. Life Is a Posthole   43
9. If You Don't Have It, Don't Fake It   46
10. Yesterday Is History   53
11. Happiness Is Plowing a Straight Row   56
12. Are We There Yet?   61
13. A Mighty Meal Begins with One Small Bite, But So
      Does Indigestion   63
14. The Face of Success   67
15. I Choose Happiness   71
16. Fun Is in Getting and Not in Having   73
17. Life's a Beach—Except for the Lifeguard   75
18. I'm Learning to Live with Affluence   81
19. Mistakes Are Stepping Stones   87
20. School Is for Children; Learning Is Forever   92
21. Revolutions Are Two-Way Streets   98
22. Love Is an Act of Obedience   102
23. The World Goes Around on Its Own—But Friends
      Grease the Axle   107
24. If I Don't Laugh at Me, Everybody Else Will   111
25. Now That I've Grown Up, My Parents Are Getting
      Smarter   114
26. God Is Smarter Than I Am   118

Acknowledgments

This is the page in the book where the author lists all the people who bragged on the manuscript before it was published. Although I couldn't really find anyone to perform that ritual, I did have some important help.

The senior writing classes of Dr. Jim Langlas of Wheaton North High School read the manuscript for me. Although I chose to reject some of their suggestions such as, "Burn it quick," and "Drop dead," I did get some excellent comments that helped make the whole thing more readable, more usable, and more fun.

To them, I owe my thanks. But you owe them some thanks, too. Without them, reading this could have been a real chore. If you want to write them, I list their names.

Pete, Scott, Christie, Richard, Michele, Dan, Jason, Dave, Bob, Tom, Arlene, Steve, Jennifer, Van, Dave, Tim, Jooney, Kurt, Dave, Chad, Anna, Kim, Kristy, Marta, Cathy, Bill, Devon, Sarah, Cathy, Scott, Nicole, Lydia, Monica, Jennifer, Brandy, Joy, Heather, Nikki, Wes, Lori, Rob, Christina, Liz, Todd.

Introduction

People who give books to graduates are probably the same people who give underwear to children for Christmas. Let's be honest. You didn't want a book. After all, you have just finished high school, and you have read about all the books you will ever need to read, and you have learned about everything you will ever need to know. Why would you want another book?

I agree with you. If I could give you a gift, I would give you a T-shirt instead of a book. But not just any T-shirt. I would give you one of those T-shirts with your philosophy of life written across its front so the whole world can see exactly what you are feeling, thinking, and believing just now.

I am a big fan of T-shirt wisdom. In fact, I am a fan of wisdom anywhere I can get it. I even enjoy locker-room wisdom, the kind that comes printed on those posters that coaches plaster around the locker room with huge globs of tape. Where else would I have learned such life-changing gems as, "When the going gets tough, the tough get going," or "Only the guy who hits the ball over the fence can loaf around the bases"?

I also enjoy classroom bulletin-board wisdom—the kind that enriches my horizons with such truths as, "Since your mother isn't here, clean up your own mess," and "Time passes; will you?" And then there's the ever popular, "If you can read this, thank a teacher." But since teachers and coaches don't change their billboards except once every decade or two, I sometimes wonder if they are really personally committed to that message or are just using those things to cover a crack in the wall.

I think that's why I especially like T-shirt wisdom. For one thing, it's mobile. It goes with you everywhere, or at least everywhere you take your chest. And besides that, you have to change it regularly or else people will hold their noses and stare at you in crowded places.

But creating a gem of wisdom that is just exactly right for a recent graduate's T-shirt is the hard part. For the full effect, the T-shirt message needs to meet four qualifications.

1. It needs to pass the "flat forehead" test. You know you have a profound shirt when people catch a glimpse of your message and slap themselves on the foreheads with the palms of their hands as if to say, "Well, why didn't I think of that?"

2. It needs to serve you as a personal challenge and goal.

3. It needs to state as accurately as possible what you are thinking and feeling at the time you're wearing it.

4. It needs to be brief enough to be written on your chest.

Now, if I am going to give you the appropriate graduation gift, my task is to come up with the perfect pithy principle that achieves those four needs.

That's a tough assignment for a couple of reasons. For one thing, I need to understand how you are responding to this whole business of graduation. But I have been working on that. During the last thirty-five years, I have met a lot of recent high-school graduates who have unloaded a heap of wisdom around me. They have asked questions and given me answers, both of which have contributed to my understanding.

My second goal then would be to put all this wisdom on a T-shirt for you. Obviously, we can't get everything on one shirt so let me propose several shirts.

Do you remember how it felt to come back to algebra class after having missed three days in a row? Everybody else was cool, collected, and confident; you were the only one around who was out to lunch.

What's the chance you're feeling a little bit like that right now? Oh, surely not. You know where you are. You have just graduated from high school. You have just finished one phase of your life and you're ready to tackle the next—with enthusiasm and assurance of success.

But maybe there *is* a little nagging question about where you are, lurking in the back of your mind. Oh, you really haven't told anybody about it; and for the most part, you've tried to ignore it. But it is still there pestering your personal peace and joy.

Since probably neither of us can put the question in exact language, let me see if I can get at it with a little three-part parable from real life.

The other day I picked up a hitchhiker. It was probably a foolish stunt, since some hitchhikers attack people. If they have a knife or a gun, they attack with that. If they don't, they attack with a sad story they have to unfold.

This guy didn't have a knife or a gun, so I got attacked with his sad story. He had been living in Michigan, out of work for months. He didn't even know where his wife or children were. But he had just received word that his mother in Arizona was ill, so he was racing across country via his thumb.

In short, this fellow is living a life of unhappiness and despair.

The other night I attended the bachelor party of a young businessman whom I have known for a while. He is finally getting married, and it is about time. For years he has been one of the leading eligible bachelors in our area. Handsome and bright, he has been tremendously successful in business, and he has the trappings that show it—a new German-made automobile and a big house. And soon he will have a lovely wife.

In short, this fellow is living a life of wealth and success.

The other morning I took my car in for some repairs and chatted with the young mechanic I have known for some time. He is not only a good mechanic but also a delightful person. He is honest and fair, but the thing I enjoy most about him is his complete dedication to his family. A few years ago he bought an old house, and he has done wonders with it. He has three children he loves, and he loves to tell you about them. He is an official in his church and is involved in Scouts with his son.

In short, this fellow is living a life of happiness and contentment.

"So what do these three people have in common?" you ask. Simple—they all graduated from high school during the same year.

Yep. They all went through the rituals. Just like you, each spent those last nine weeks of the senior year trying to determine how little work he could do and still pass. (Come on, admit it. You didn't do flip those last nine weeks.) Each one of them checked out that cap and gown, rushed home, tried it on in front of the mirror, and then spent the next several days trying to decide how to look good in that rig.

Each of them attended the graduation rehearsal where some uptight sponsors made too big a deal out of something as insignificant as "Whatever you do, don't forget your number. If you forget your number, well, you may not even get to graduate."

Each of them attended the graduation exercises, listened to some speaker (who hadn't been their age in so long he had forgotten how it was) say to all those eager young graduates, "Now when you get out into real life . . ." while the graduates themselves sit there thinking, *If this isn't real life, where have I been for the past eighteen years, Mars?*

Each one walked across the stage, shook hands with some official-looking person from the school board, grabbed that diploma, and went into a fit of frenzy, throwing hats and jumping around.

Each one hugged all the relatives who lived close enough to come, posed for more pictures than ever before, attended at least three all-night parties, slept past noon the next day, and woke up with a strange feeling that something very important had just happened to him, but he wasn't sure what.

And now for your burning question—the one you have been trying in vain to avoid these past few weeks. Ten years after high-school graduation, what's the difference between a hitchhiker traveling across the country via thumb and a successful businessman traveling along in a German-made automobile? Ten years after high-school graduation, what's the difference between a life of happiness and contentment and a life of despair?

I'm sure that you have pondered this, and if you haven't,

you should. It is what new high-school graduates think about, or at least what the thoughtful ones think about, whether they admit it or not.

Sure, this is a time for frivolity and celebration. But it is more than that. It is also a time for some rather serious thinking about God, yourself, the world, and your future in it. In other words, where are you?

Let's look at this thought from another angle.

Life is one transition after another. That is the gist of human existence. I suppose the first major transition is just being born, but since we don't have much to do with that event, it really doesn't count as an achievement. Sometime when we are babies we burble something that sounds remotely like "Mama," and our proud parents run all over the neighborhood telling friends and relatives that we have just learned to talk. That's a transition.

We start to school, and that's a transition. We learn to read. We go to junior high. We have our first date. We get our first kiss. We graduate. We get a job. We get married and have children. Our children have children. We retire. We die. Like I said, life is just one transition after another.

You can look at all those transitions like you look at a plate of spinach. You can dread and hate it if you want to, but you are still going to have to tackle it. So you may as well look at a transition (and a plate of spinach) as a challenge and an opportunity. That's the way to good health.

As you have already realized, those transitions are more than just fleeting moments that come and go. They mark major changes in our lives, in our attitudes, and in our thoughts. In fact, the changes are so significant and powerful that one of those "ologist" types (I think this one was a sociologist) wrote a book called *Passages,* which is supposed to tell people how to manage their lives through periods of major change.

But of all the passages we face in a lifetime, there isn't one more significant or abrupt than that transition called high-school graduation.

For one thing, it slips up on you. Here you are living the life of a high-school student, which is for the most part a controlled existence. Someone tells you when to get up and when to go to bed. Someone tells you when to go to class, not just once but six times a day. Someone tells you when to go to study hall, what to study, and what will happen to you if you don't.

In the midst of all this, you cry out for any little bit of independence you can grab. You fantasize about a time in the distant future when you can make your own decisions and direct your own life. But you still run through the halls to get to the next class on time and stay up half the night cramming to learn the stuff that someone ordered you to learn on the grounds that it is important to you.

About the time you decide that this is going to be the nature of the rest of your life, you graduate from high school, and the whole transition takes only about an hour, picture-taking time included. They kick you out of that place, and all of a sudden you discover the burden of the blessing of freedom. You find that you have to make a ton of decisions that could have a permanent impact on your life, you have to make them right away, and you probably sense that you are going to have to make those decisions by yourself.

Be honest. You aren't ready for this. No one ever told you that the price of freedom was the loneliness of making all those decisions. And you definitely aren't prepared to do it. So then you run in search of those people who just a couple days ago were quite willing to control your life completely, and they aren't a bit of help.

They give you a half-baked smile that is supposed to communicate their confidence in you, and they say something shallow, "Well, just do whatever you think is best. After all, it is your life." Where is a little control now that you could use it?

At this point, you may argue that you can delay this abrupt transition of high-school graduation by just choosing more school. If you pick college or trade school, or even the military, you are just trading one form of control for another; or in simple terms, you are just trading controllers.

But it isn't all that simple. Regardless of what you do following high school, you are still going to have to make some significant decisions affecting your future. You are going to have to set some goals, and you are going to have to determine how you are going to go about chasing those goals.

Of course, high-school graduation isn't the first transition you have been through. But it is probably the first one you have survived since you had sense enough to know what was happening to you. When you started first grade, you didn't know what you were getting into. You might have felt some twinges of sadness that you were leaving home for the day, but you really didn't know what was going to rise up to take its place. When you moved to junior high school, you probably felt a little shock wave and might have even cried yourself to sleep a couple of nights, but you still didn't quite put it all together.

But for this high-school thing, you are fully alert. You have all your wits about you. You know where you have been, but the only thing you know about where you are going is that you are going into your future, wherever that might be.

Another problem with this transition from high school to the rest of your life is that you don't really know how you are supposed to feel about it all. Part of you wants to celebrate and jump for joy. And why not? High school isn't easy. You have made a major achievement. You are pleased with yourself for what you have accomplished, and you are bubbling over with enthusiasm for what lies ahead. Everybody you meet is encouraging you to celebrate. So you do.

But that's the public side, the side that you let everybody see. On the other hand, the private side, the one only you can see, still has its fears and worries and concerns. So at times you celebrate and that's honest. But at other times, you weep a bit and cringe some. And that is honest, too. All the while, you are frustrated by mixed emotions. You just wish you could respond honestly in one way and be done with all this ambiguity.

But that's just the trouble with transitions. They always come with at least two sets of feelings. That's why you need to wear that announcement about transitions on your T-shirt— just to let people know what you are going through.

Transition means change, and that's what is happening to you right now. There are two ways to handle change. You can just let it happen and hang on for the ride, or you can actually take charge of the change.

Taking charge of change is called making a decision.

Decisions! Decisions! Decisions!

You have probably heard that word so much in recent weeks that you have grown a bit tired of it and maybe even a little frightened. Everybody you meet is pressing you for some kind of decision: "Well, now that you have been finished with high school for at least two weeks, have you picked a college yet? Have you chosen your life's career for the next forty-seven years? Are you engaged yet? What are you planning to name your children? Do you have any money invested in a retirement fund? Have you chosen a burial plot?"

All those decisions to make, and you don't even know whether you want pizza or tacos for lunch.

It doesn't take long to realize that making decisions is hard work. You have to shut out the world and think. You have to make yourself lonely so you can do it yourself. And after all that, you still don't know how the decision is going to work out in the long run.

You may be tempted to argue that it may be better not to make a decision at all. "Where's the place of faith?" you may want to ask. "We have God's grace, God's protection, and God's plan. Maybe we should leave our future up to chance so that God can do His work."

But the problem with that thinking is that God gave each of us a mind, and we use our minds for three functions.

1. We use our minds to come to a full acceptance of the gifts and talents God has given us. The talents are a gift from God, but we need to have an honest understanding of what they are.

2. We use our minds to realize what we could become with our gifts so that we can best fulfill God's purpose and glorify Him.

3. We use our minds to determine what we must do to become what God wants us to be.

In other words, we make decisions. We gather information; we sort through it; we list the possibilities; we weigh each one; and after all that, we plan an action.

It's tiring just thinking about it. That's why you need to wear the shirt. In implied language it says, "Get out of my way. Leave me alone. Don't interrupt. I'm working as hard as I can. I'm making a decision."

And that's probably your most important job just now.

If you are typical, the one decision that seems to be most demanding of your attention is the question of more school. Shall you continue in school, and if so, what kind of school should you pursue? I don't want to minimize that decision because it is very important, but I am not going to get into a full-blown discussion for a couple of reasons. For one thing, there are books and experts giving you all sorts of advice about those particular questions: Should you go to college? Where should you go to college? What should you major in? Should you be a cheerleader your freshman year? If you need more information concerning those decisions, you will surely want to read those books or contact those experts. They can give you more comprehensive advice than we can get on a T-shirt message.

But the other reason I am going to avoid discussing the decision of college is that it might throw you off course. If you can get caught up in that decision about college and use all of your available energy and time confronting that, you can avoid even thinking about some other really significant changes, perhaps even earthshaking ones that are going to take place in your world in the next four years regardless of whether or not you spend that time in school.

Here's a rather startling thought. At the end of that time, you will be four years older than you are now. Isn't that an earthshaking piece of information? But I am actually very serious. I want you to think about that and what it means. Who are you going to be in four years?

To get a perspective of how long four years actually is, let's look back. Four years ago you were a freshman. You were probably frightened, running about the halls of the school, scared to death of the seniors, the teachers, and especially the principal. You probably weren't overly confident in the presence of the opposite sex, either. You didn't know your way around school. You didn't know what courses to take or with whom to eat lunch. In other words, you were a freshman.

Now look at you and how you have changed: confident, poised, and on top of things—or at least you are at school. If you like this little game of looking back, let me suggest that you try to find something that you wrote four years ago when you were just a freshman. (Maybe your mother still has something stuck on the refrigerator door from that period.) Read that and ask yourself if you can even remotely remember the person who scribbled those words. One thing you will realize when you look back is that you have changed.

Now try to look into the future the same distance—just four years. You have to realize that you are going to undergo some changes in that period of time, too. Those are the changes we want to consider.

For one thing, regardless of where you spend the next four years, in that period of time you will move from adolescence to adulthood. You may want to protest that I shouldn't call you an adolescent now, but that's what you are. And you may want to protest that you don't want to become an adult, but that's just what happens to a person who quits being seventeen and becomes twenty-one. People call you an adult, whether you are ready for it or not. This is going to happen, and you need to think about it. You need to prepare yourself to make some decisions.

Since the changes you will encounter in the next few years will come in three general areas, the decisions will come in three areas as well. Let's look at them.

Changes in yourself. Because we have already talked about this, I won't dwell on it in detail lest I frighten you completely. But I want to remind you again that high-school graduation is a signal event indicating that you are going to undergo some major changes in your personhood. Although you may not change some of your characteristics and even basic beliefs, you will change nonetheless. You need to know that because if you don't deal with it consciously, you may wake up one day four or five years later to discover that you have become somebody that you don't know and maybe don't even like.

Changes in career. Thus far in your life your career has been preparation. I use the word *career* intentionally. Preparing yourself is indeed a valuable, worthwhile career, and the fact that you have graduated from high school says that you have done it well.

But now that you have finished high school, your career will become performance. That may not happen overnight, but you are in the process of moving from preparation to performance. That means you will need to make some important decisions about issues like success and how to obtain it.

Changes in relationships. You have probably already begun to realize that this is going to happen. During those graduation night parties, you went around hugging all your friends and promising to stay in touch with them for the rest of your life when all the time you knew in the back of your mind that you would never see some of those people again. Yes, you are going to change your friends, and the way you go about getting friends will change, too.

You will also change your relationship with your parents. Moving from adolescence to adulthood makes that kind of change necessary. In addition to all that, you will probably move away from home sometime in the next few years. You may even choose a spouse and become a parent yourself. All these events will affect your relationship with your parents, and you need to be on top of it.

You will also find that your relationship with God will change. That is the nature of our relationship with God—it changes. It is supposed to grow, but whether it does or not is one result of your ability to make decisions.

I like that outline. Let's use it as an organizational scheme for the rest of the T-shirts that I offer you as graduation gifts. Some of them will tell stories about the changes in you as a person. Some will broadcast to the world your thoughts about changes in your career, and some will announce that you have taken charge of the changes in your relationships.

That sounds like a rather exhausting schedule, doesn't it? That's why you need this particular shirt.

Maybe it will buy you some space to ponder those decisions.

GOD LOVES SPUNK

Since spunk is one of those highfalutin intellectual words that probably doesn't get covered in most run-of-the-mill dictionaries, let me offer my definition here.

spunk *n:* The ability of a person to make the most out of what God has given him/her.

Let me explain that with some illustrations.

The other day, a fortysomething-year-old man told me about his Sunday school experience during his elementary years. Only two boys were in the class, but they were such terrors that teachers assigned to the class were drawing combat pay on the side. Finally, one very patient man took on the responsibility of herding the rascals, and he kept the class for three years in a row.

The man telling me the story was making the point of the value of a good teacher in our young impressionable lives. But there was another point hidden just under the surface of the original story. That man telling me the story in the first place is now a highly esteemed pastor of a large church and is widely recognized as a faithful servant of God. And the other half of the notorious Sunday school class is now a missionary in Africa somewhere.

Do you see my point? God isn't intimidated by a little enthusiasm. Sometimes humans assigned the responsibility of controlling the enthusiastic feel like running away and hiding, but God isn't intimidated.

The Scriptures are filled with examples. Let's try Paul, just because his name is simple and I can write it without checking the spelling in the Bible.

Paul (or Saul, as he was known in his earlier life) was not doing good things, but he was doing bad enthusiastically. He was persecuting all those new Christians, and he was doing it with great zest. So God converted him. In a dramatic scene, God met Paul on the road to Damascus, and God changed his heart, his direction, and his mission; but He didn't change Paul's enthusiasm.

Paul went from enthusiastically destroying the church to building up the church with just as much enthusiasm. The mission was God's, but the enthusiasm was still Paul's. That's what I call spunk.

You can find the same thing in a whole bevy of biblical characters—Jacob, Joseph, Moses, Joshua, Caleb, Ruth, Esther, David, and even Peter. Each one took personal ability and a set of circumstances and turned the situation into something positive for self and for God's kingdom. That is spunk, and that's what it takes to drive instead of thumb yourself through life. Spunk is the product of a specific decision.

Of course, things are never quite as easy as they sound at first. When you think of your spunk here, you are probably already convinced that this is exactly what you want, but let me warn you. You may have to battle a bit to get there.

If spunk were just a simple little achievement that comes along naturally in the course of everyday activity, everybody would have it. But that isn't so. To live with spunk, you have to fight some monsters. And you have to fight them frequently throughout your life. Let's take a look at three of them.

1. I WISH I HAD. . . .

This monster is the most popular of negative thinking and a big hurdle facing spunk. I hear it in high schools every day: "I wish I had that guy's brains." "She is so pretty. I'm envious." "No matter how hard I work I will never be as good in sports as she is." "Why does everybody in class understand it except me?" "What would I have to have to get a date?" "I could never be a doctor. I don't have the brains." The list goes on. And each thought is a destructive one.

The problem here is that we focus on what we don't have instead of what we do have. The solution is simple. You should just sit down with your pencil in hand and make a list of all your strong points. In the process of creating you, what specific gifts did God give you? In the process of living, what specific lessons have you learned?

Making that list should be simple, but the problem with making a list of our strong points is that we are always tempted to compare our strong points with someone else's, and when we do that, we always are going to come out short, which leads us back to that old monster, I WISH I HAD. . . . It's a vicious whirlpool, and once we get trapped in it, we are constantly pulled to the middle.

The only hope is to break loose completely. Models may be important here. Take Paul again for an example. According to what we can piece together in the Scriptures, Paul lived a completely exciting life, full of adventure, travel, and intrigue, and he accomplished tremendous achievements. But also according to what we can piece together from the Scriptures, Paul would have never been asked to play a private detective on television. He just wasn't as handsome as a Thomas Magnum or a Remington Steele.

I suppose he could have let that bother him, but there is no indication that he did. There is no indication that he ever stopped and said, "Oh, Lord, why couldn't I have been as handsome as Barnabas? Why couldn't I have been as persuasive as Peter or as charming as Silas or whatever?"

He didn't waste time fighting the monster of I WISH I HAD. . . . Instead he used his energy fighting other monsters and was far more effective in God's purpose because of it.

Paul teaches a big lesson. The talent you lack is not keeping you from accomplishing something. Your handicap is not having the spunk to use what you do have.

2. MAYBE SOMEBODY ELSE COULD.

This monster is a child of the first one. Once you convince yourself that you don't have what it takes and someone else does, the next step is easy. You just say, "I'll let someone else do it. After all, that person would surely be better at it than I am."

With this kind of thinking, you go through life filled with ideas about what you could do, the accomplishments you could achieve, and the contributions you could make. But you never quite get around to doing anything because you always have that gnawing thought that someone else could do it better.

But that is just the problem. No one else does it. Even if someone else could do it better, it still isn't getting done. Through the years, I've noticed two distinct types of people: Those people who do things, and those people who sit around and criticize those who do things. Now you figure out which ones are leading lives of success and contentment.

My friend tells a story. Many years ago he visited Hannibal, Missouri, the boyhood home of that very fine writer Mark Twain. One morning as my friend sat on a park bench facing the Mississippi River, he imagined the scenes from the various books, and he delighted in the contribution that Twain had made with his writings. An elderly man came and sat with my friend that morning. He, too, was a native of Hannibal, Missouri, having lived there for more than eighty years. He, too, knew regional stories of quaint characters and bizarre situations. He, too, could tell a story with a flair that riveted the listener. But he wasn't famous. No one outside Hannibal had ever heard of the old man. The difference between him and Mark Twain was not in the stories, because they both knew the same stories. Nor was it necessarily in the ability to tell the stories, because both were good at that. The difference between the two was that Twain wrote his stories down.

I tell you this story so it will be a constant reminder to both of us. Throughout your life you are going to be threatened by that monster, MAYBE SOMEBODY ELSE COULD. He will tackle nearly every good idea you will ever have. He will steal your spunk. But when he does come, just remember that Twain wrote the stories down.

3. WHAT IF THEY LAUGH?

This monster is the most treacherous of all. Now confess. You have already been attacked by him on occasions. You have probably caught yourself saying, "I would really like to try out for cheerleader, but what would happen if I didn't make it?" "I wonder what the teacher would say if I wrote what I really want to write on this paper?" "I would really like to comb my hair this way, but nobody else is doing it, so I won't, either."

Don't kid yourself into thinking that this monster attacks only high-school people. This guy is dangerous throughout a lifetime. Unless we are consciously aware of the danger of this kind of thinking and work to overcome it, we will go through life always asking ourselves before we start any project, "What will people think?"

Not long ago I met a man in his mid-twenties who had just enrolled in a special school to learn to be an undertaker. As we talked, I became impressed that the fellow was thoroughly excited about what he was learning and how he would someday be able to use all that in his work.

In the course of our conversation I asked him how long he had been interested in becoming an undertaker.

"Oh, a long time," he reported. "This is what I've wanted to do since I was a freshman in high school."

"So why are you just getting into the school?" I asked, thinking that maybe there was an age restriction on that kind of training.

"Up until just recently," he said with a hint of joy in his voice, "I would have been too embarrassed to tell my friends what I was doing." And then I understood his excitement. He had just whipped a monster, a monster that otherwise would have robbed him of his spunk.

Well, there you have it. Those are some of the enemies that could keep you from becoming everything that God has made you to be. God has already begun His work in you. You can see that. Now your job is to promise God that you'll meet the challenge.

That's why I would give you this particular T-shirt at this time. As you wear it down the street announcing to the world that God loves spunk, it also reminds you of what you have to do.

But it is also something of a statement of your academic achievement. You now know a highfalutin intellectual word.

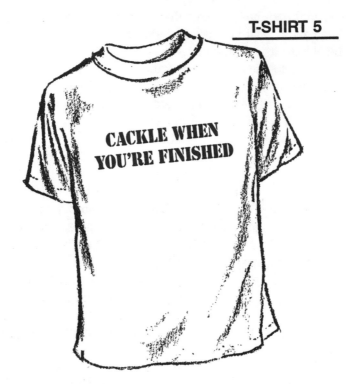

Before you dismiss this piece of wisdom as being totally silly and throw the whole T-shirt into the back of the drawer never to be seen again, let me give you a simple little test.

TEST: Name something that lays eggs. Quickly, give me the first thing that pops into your mind.

Did you ever stop to ponder the fact that a really good chicken lays about 250 eggs a year while an average mama fish lays about a million eggs a year? Based on that little tidbit, why did you say a chicken as an answer to my test question?

I know why. The chicken has a better public relations department. It's all in advertisement and salesmanship. That mama fish lays a million eggs and never says a word—not even a peep. In all my life, I've never heard a fish peep.

On the other hand, every time a chicken lays just one egg

she cackles enough to wake up the whole neighborhood. That's publicity—acknowledging your accomplishments.

Now bragging at the top of your lungs like the chicken does may be carrying things a little too far, but there is absolutely nothing wrong with accepting your own achievements. I realize that a factor of humility is involved here, but humility is simply the art of letting someone else brag about your accomplishments. Common sense says you really need to know when you have finished a job and have done it well.

Personally, I like mowing the lawn. Well, that isn't true just the way I said it. I like to be finished mowing the lawn. I start mowing, and at every point in the process, I know how much I have covered and how much is left; and I definitely know when I have finished. At this point, tired, sweaty, and out of breath, I look back over that fine-looking newly mowed sod, and I cackle. I know what I have just accomplished, and I am satisfied with myself for having achieved it.

You need those kinds of finishing spots in your life. If you don't have them, you lose out on a vital component of good mental health—the feeling of accomplishment.

Now I tell you all this because I want you to come to a full appreciation of the significant accomplishment in your life. You have just finished high school, and that is a big deal. Oh, I hear the critics who would downplay your achievement. People my age, like your parents and teachers, will tell you that high school is just not as tough as it used to be in the good old days before we were spoiled with things like television, computers, school buses, and warm weather in winter. Politicians will tell you that as American students you didn't work nearly as hard or suffer nearly as much as the Japanese students do and by all rights you really ought to be ashamed of yourself for taking it all so easy. If you're not careful you may even find yourself getting trapped in this "let's downplay high school" game, and say to yourself, "If it is such a big deal, why did so many people make it?"

But I am here to assure you that graduating from high

school is a major accomplishment, and you ought to be prepared to cackle a bit about it. I will even go further than that. In the past thirty-five years since I finished school, I have come to realize that going to high school—and doing it successfully—is one of the most exhausting and difficult challenges we will ever undertake. If you have what it takes to make it through high school, you have what it takes to achieve practically any goal you aspire to.

Now let's take a look at some personal strengths you need just to survive one day of high school. I really hate to do this so soon after graduation because it may bring back some unpleasant memories, but I do it for two reasons. I want you to realize that high school was indeed a tough assignment, and I want to assure you that you will probably not have to go through it again.

Since you have just finished high school and are probably still agog about outlines, I will develop all this in outline form for simple study should this appear on a quiz later.

I. Perseverance, commonly known as stick-to-itiveness. This is a prominent personality trait for success in any endeavor, and it is particularly valuable in the physically active professions such as professional sports and parenthood. It is one of the chief features of a high-school graduate, appearing in several forms.
   A. The Enduring Seat. Anyone who can sit in those plastic school desks for six hours a day quietly enough to please a hard-line teacher merits a place in the Perseverance Hall of Fame.
   B. The Vacuum Cleaner Brain. I visit high-school classrooms every day, and in every class I pick up at least thirty-five pieces of new information. When you multiply that times the number of classes you have each day, it comes out to a bunch of new information. I have decided that high-school students have better brains than I do or they aren't paying attention.

C. Bladder Control. Enough said on this topic, except most adults don't realize that you often went a full half-day before you earned a bathroom stop.

D. Quick Jaws. In no other line of work is a person expected to wait in a cafeteria line twenty minutes of a thirty-minute lunch break and scarf it all down in five minutes.

E. Late Night Comprehension. I'll let you in on a little secret. Many successful people in a variety of professions never have homework, much less homework requiring alert mental composition after midnight.

F. Happy Feet. I do not have the words to explain how thousands of high-school students can move through halls in near-riot conditions just to get to the next class on time. And they do it every hour. My only suggestion is happy feet. If you finished your senior year with fewer than five tardies, you have just demonstrated a virtue that could propel you to great heights.

II. Adaptability. The ability to make quick adjustments to new circumstances is a prized personality trait because it reflects one's ability to analyze others as well as oneself. The very nature of the high-school day not only requires this but teaches it as well. The truly successful high-school student is indeed an expert in adaptability in various forms.

A. On Cue Laughter. Some teachers actually have a fair sense of humor and often say something funny. Other teachers just think they have a sense of humor. In either case, the student must master the art of laughing appropriately.

B. Personal Whim Catering. One teacher wants your name in the upper left hand corner; another wants it on the back. One teacher wants you to talk in class and grades you down if you don't; another wants complete silence. One teacher lets you sit where you want; another assigns seats. And if you ever dare ask a teacher, "Why?" you get the standard intellectual answer, "Because that's the way I want it," and so you learn to adapt. In a profession, you would call that skill public relations ability.

C. Instantly Adjustable Body Clocks. You are supposed to have science the first period of the day and eat lunch at 12:07, but on the days that you have pep assemblies, you have science the last period of the day and eat lunch at 10:16. But that's no big deal. You just make the switches in your mind and body clock. But did you ever notice how such changes throw the teachers into a state of shock? Something as insignificant as a fire drill in the hour you were supposed to have a quiz seems to ruin their whole day.

Regardless of what you may or may not have learned in high school about such things as geography, literature, or French, the fact that you made it indicates that you at least developed the skills of perseverance and adaptability.

You have achieved something significant. You have mastered a very difficult task. I, for one, salute you.

Wear your T-shirt with confidence. You may even want to stop and cackle once in a while. Just try to do it when you are among friends. Some folks may not understand.

I like this little piece of wisdom. It gets right to the heart of abundant living. Lest you accuse me of being lazy, let me assure you that I actually learned it reading the Scriptures. Yes, that's right. This is biblical. You can find it in John 21.

One day the disciples found themselves facing a real crisis. Three years before, they had given up nearly everything that had been a foundation for their lives to follow this leader Jesus Christ. They gave up their jobs, their status in the union, their retirement benefits, their spot in the community and in religious circles and, in some ways, their own families.

But that wasn't really a bad bargain, as long as Jesus was still around. They had food, health insurance, a good company of friends, and some rather serious work to keep them occupied. And they had a powerful, dynamic leader. In the midst of all this, they had to have some sense that they were involved in something significant, real, and permanent.

But then one day, that all-powerful leader was executed, crucified like a common criminal. And the world tumbled around them.

So there they were—without a leader and without direction. About that time, Christ Himself came back from the tomb and gave the disciples a whole new challenge. They realized they couldn't go back to where they had been three years before. And they also realized that they had just inherited the whole mission of Christ. They had to take action; they had to do the right thing; and they had to do it now.

So how did they respond to this urgent call to action? They went fishing. You don't believe it? Look it up.

While they were out there, they met Christ, ate a good breakfast, reaffirmed their mission, and got their act together. Then, and not until then, were they ready to roll up their sleeves and tackle the long job ahead.

I give you this little reminder as a bit of assurance because I suspect that you feel you are about to discover the definition of the rat race.

You've heard of the rat race before. Your parents talk about it; teachers talk about it. But you always thought it was punishment inflicted on old people—commuting in traffic, keeping appointments, hustling to make a dollar—and all this time you have wondered why anyone would spend a life chasing rats.

But now you have begun to find you have your own forms of the old rat race. It's those people asking if you have made all those decisions yet, in such a tone that just by asking you it sounds as if they are accusing you of wasting the best years of your life.

It's the car salesman insisting that if you don't drive it home right now someone else is going to grab it up in the next three minutes. It's rushing to finish one hectic world of high school with all the classes and papers and finals and graduation exercises piled in too little time and then being hurled headfirst into another hectic world of a demanding decision-making process while you are still actively involved in trying to live a normal life.

It's rush, rush, rush! There are two ways for you to respond to all that rushing. You could just plunge right in, lose yourself in mad activity, and chase rats the rest of your life.

Or you could go fishing. (Since you have just finished senior lit, you have realized by now that I am using fishing here as a symbol. I won't insult your high degree of education by telling you what a symbol is. Nor will I insult you by explaining what fishing is a symbol of. You figured that out two pages ago.)

It doesn't take Einstein to determine which of these is the most popular option. We are living in an age of activity. We put a much higher price on the virtue of busyness than on the virtue of thoughtfulness. Have you noticed that in recent years, church groups don't go on retreats? They now go on "advances," as if there is something spiritually suspect about taking a weekend off to do nothing but think, and maybe pray.

But I want to put in a plea for fishing. There is something to be said about the value of thinking. Thinking takes time and sometimes demands some isolation.

The poet Wordsworth once said, "Poetry is the spontaneous overflow of powerful feelings." Well, from what I have heard hanging around the halls of high schools lately, I have come to believe that most of us would find that "profanity is the spontaneous overflow of powerful feelings."

But Wordsworth put another stipulation on his observation. He said, "Poetry is the spontaneous overflow of powerful feelings, recollected in tranquillity." That's the difference, that little hint of tranquillity. And finding those spots of tranquillity may well be the difference between a life of beauty and a profane life.

At least the disciples found their fishing trip valuable. They went out to the Sea of Galilee not really knowing what they were supposed to do or how to go about doing it. In modern language, you might say that they hadn't "found themselves" yet.

But while they were out there far away from the mad rush of their responsibility, they met Christ. Let's define that. It means worshiping Christ; speaking with Him; dealing with our inadequacies, our fears, our apprehensions; and getting the vision that gives us the direction, courage, and the enthusiasm to make decisions and carry them out.

These are valuable moments in our lives. No—let me make that stronger. These are *necessary* moments in our lives.

Obviously, we don't have to go fishing for months at a time, but we do need to make sure we have some method for getting off by ourselves to check out what's in our own minds and see how that matches with what we can learn about the mind of Christ.

These moments are particularly important to you just now. As the disciples taught us in their little fishing trip, worship is the starting point for tackling transitions, changes, and the pressures of decision making. But for some reason, now that these moments are most essential to you, you may find yourself having a hard time grabbing some of them.

During high school you could at least daydream in class, especially after you learned the art of looking interested. And you probably had a lot of other down moments during the day to think your thoughts, make your plans, dream your dreams, and get on better terms with God.

But after high school is over and you get into that mad rush of chasing rats, you may find yourself at times wanting to scream out for just a few seconds of peace.

That's what this T-shirt message is about. Look at it as a silent scream.

I'M NOT AFRAID
TO CATCH WHAT
I'M CHASING

Let's talk about what you are chasing. For illustration, let me tell you a story about my life as a big-game hunter. It began one day when I was in college—and ended the same day.

I was home for Thanksgiving break when I met an old friend one evening. In the course of our conversation he said, "I'll tell you what we should do for some real fun. Let's go duck hunting!" Now I had never been duck hunting before. In fact, I had never been any kind of hunting before, unless trapping mice would count. But that did sound like fun—something the guys would do, something macho and daring. So I accepted the invitation.

In preparation, I borrowed my father's gun and one shell. As far as I knew I was as well armed as any hunter who ever made a safari.

At 4:00 A.M. my friend came banging on my door. I'm sure you realize that college students don't usually get up at 4:00 A.M. when they are home on break. In fact, college students don't usually get up in the A.M. at all when they are on break. But I got up because I knew that we were going to have some fun, and I will do about anything stupid to have fun.

We traveled for miles in his pickup truck, and I fought sleep every inch of the way. You know how it is. It's like going to class the hour after lunch. My head hurt from trying to keep my eyes open, and my neck got sore from jerking myself awake so often. But I was having a good time.

Finally, he pulled the truck alongside the road and stopped.

"What are we doing?" I asked. "I thought we were going to the river."

"We are," he said, with what I detected as a hint of glee in his voice. "But we have to walk from here."

"How far?" I wanted to know.

"About a mile and a half," he said, forgetting to add that it was through plowed ground.

Now for you neophytes, I need to explain that walking through plowed ground is not one of the most attractive ways to spend an early morning. Plowed ground is worse than water. It gets into your shoes and squishes up around your toes and turns your feet red. Besides that, we walked through tall weeds, and the seeds fell into our faces and down the backs of our shirts and itched.

So I was duck hunting. I was tired. I had dirt in my shoes and itchy seeds in my shirt. It was probably the most fun I'd ever had in my life.

Just as we got close enough to see the river and I had decided that maybe I could live through this after all, my friend said, "Shssh."

And I said, "What do you mean, shssh?"

And he said, "We have to crawl the rest of the way into the blind."

That's when I realized we were standing in the backwater of

the river. I'm sure you know about that stuff. It rains and settles in there. After a while, as it gets dirtier and dirtier, it turns green and takes on a life of its own. That's when it turns to smelly slime. That morning, we got down on our hands and knees and crawled through that smelly slime into the duck blind.

We sat in the blind in a dizzy stupor for what seemed like eternity. About daybreak, one lone duck flew up from across the river. Without even thinking, I lifted my gun, closed both eyes, and pulled the trigger. And that duck came falling down. I don't think I hit him with the shot. I think he must have heard the gun go off, had a heart attack, and died. Nonetheless, he tumbled out of the sky and fell into the icy cold river.

I took my clothes off, went into that icy water, retrieved the duck, took him home (where my mother cooked him), and ate him. That's when I realized something important: I hate duck.

Now that's the message of this T-shirt. Don't spend your life chasing what you wouldn't want if you caught it.

Jesus said it a different way when He told us, "Do not lay up for yourselves treasures on earth, where moth and rust destroy and where thieves break in and steal; but lay up for yourselves treasures in heaven, where neither moth nor rust destroys and where thieves do not break in and steal" (Matt. 6:19–20).

You have probably already seen the results of this kind of thinking, since it is common in schools. People often say, "I just want those people to like me, and I'll do anything to get it to happen." Then they do whatever they think it takes to earn someone's friendship, and they wind up doubly disappointed. They are disappointed with what it costs them to earn the friendship, and they are also disappointed with the friendship when they finally earn it. It just wasn't worth the effort.

The other day I parked my car in the junior-high-school parking lot and sat watching the crowd that gathers across the street to smoke during the lunch period. They seemed to be a fairly normal group, but one girl attracted my attention. Like the rest of them, she was smoking a cigarette, but every time she took a puff, she coughed, wheezed, turned blue, and almost passed out. It was apparent to me that she wasn't enjoying smoking at all. The uninformed might ask why she was doing it in the first place. But the answer was obvious—she had to smoke. That was the price she paid for the right to stand with that bunch during the lunch period. In other words, that was the price she had to pay to chase whatever it was she was chasing. I hope for her sake that she is going to be satisfied with her goal when she finally reaches it, but I fear she won't be. The cost is too great for the results.

Because there is so much of this kind of activity in school life, we might get the idea that this is a problem facing young people. But that isn't necessarily so. I see people of every age investing all their time and energy chasing some phantom that is supposed to bring instant joy and happiness. Yet some time later they end up in frustration and despair, with empty dreams.

As I said, high-school students put forth effort to have friends. And that's noble. But at what cost?

Frequently I meet college students who are spending their energies and time trying to make good grades. And that's noble. But at what cost?

Often I meet parents who work long and hard to provide their children with all the material advantages of life. And that's noble. But at what cost?

I once had an old dog who spent his whole life chasing cars. That was the only form of entertainment he allowed himself. I suppose that was noble. But he would have had no idea what to do with a car if he had ever caught one. That's the problem.

I know this all sounds serious and somber, but the solution to it is really simple. Just make sure you like duck before you waste your life hunting for one.

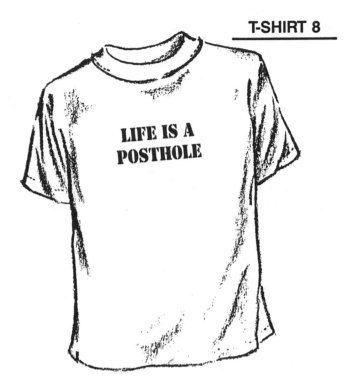

It took me thirty-five years to learn this lesson, beginning on the night of my own high-school graduation. I had actually looked forward to that event. Because I have always been a sentimental old romanticist, I was rather excited about dressing up in that funny-looking garb and marching to the tune of "Pomp and Circumstance."

Besides, I got to give a speech. I remember standing in front of those people and speaking as if I really had something important to say. And when I finished, they clapped, either because they were courteous or because they were sincerely glad that I had finished my speech. But I felt important.

Later people came to congratulate me and wish me good luck and even take my picture. And again I felt important.

That very night I decided I had finally figured out the meaning of life. This was it: going to graduation exercises, basking in all that attention, feeling important. And I went to bed having solved the mystery of the universe.

The next morning, my father, without consideration for my newfound wisdom, awakened me early and shipped me off to a remote corner of our ranch to spend the whole day digging postholes.

During the thirty-five years that followed, I have learned that life is more like digging postholes than it is going to graduation exercises.

I hope you have in front of you a life filled with earthshaking experiences and memorable moments. I hope that the rest of your life is even more exciting than high school was—but I wouldn't count on it.

For many of you during high school, life seems to leap from one mountaintop to the next. Every time you turn around you are looking forward to the big game or the big date or the big test or the big party or even those once-in-a-lifetime affairs like the SAT test, prom, or graduation. There is always something just ahead of you to anticipate—to quicken your pulse, shorten your breath and tense your hair follicles. Oh, some of those moments may seem a little frightening at times, and you face some of them with some fear and apprehension and even dread. But they do break up the routine.

Life beyond high school doesn't have those same kinds of mountaintops to leap toward. Sometimes life almost has an even character to it.

Let me illustrate. I remember one of the big dates in my life. It was the first time I had ever had a breakfast date. I had had dinner dates where we had gone out for a footlong and milk shake, but I had never had a breakfast date.

It was during the spring of one of my college years. I went wandering across campus absorbed in the smell of the flowers, the lush green grass, and the early morning dew. Some birds came by and chirped me a song.

The young lady who shared this fine morning with me came

out of her dormitory wearing a frilly frock that danced in the gentle breezes. She wore a hint of perfume, and her hair was immaculately coiffured. And we went to breakfast.

Since then I have had a breakfast date with that same little girl 10,950 days in a row. No early morning dew. No birds chirping. No frilly frocks. No hint of perfume. No immaculately coiffured hairdo. Just me and the lady. But the proof of my love for her is that I find her more exciting now than I found her that morning thirty years ago.

That's the message of postholes, and it applies to every area of my life.

I have a friend who taught high-school biology in the same room for thirty-three years in a row and never missed a day. When he finally retired, he missed the excitement of it all. That's the kind of test I'm talking about—the test of our ability to find excitement and thrill in the everyday and in the seeming sameness of our tasks.

In high school, the events themselves provide some excitement. After you get out of high school, that excitement comes from your personality, or it doesn't come at all.

Frankly, I'm a little tired of people complaining that they are bored. They are bored with their jobs or their spouses or their cars or their houses or their lives. For one thing, it seems almost blasphemous to say such a thing. It's almost as if they are yelling at God for not making the world exciting enough.

But the big lesson to remember is that being bored is a statement about the person rather than about the circumstances. This is one of the first lessons you will have to learn as a high-school graduate. In fact, one of the biggest decisions you will have to make is the decision not to be bored, regardless of what's happening to you.

And I say it this way because I want you to realize that it is your decision. Once you have made that decision, don't be afraid to advertise it. Wear it on your T-shirt for all to see.

IF YOU DON'T
HAVE IT: DON'T
FAKE IT

This particular piece of T-shirt wisdom has a double message; in other words, it's a transition. (You learned about transitions in writing class. Those are the little devices we use to get from here to there.) It has something quite significant to say about you as a person. But it also has something to say about your career.

Quite often when you prepare for the great earthshaking career that offers job satisfaction, lifetime happiness, personal fulfillment, and a German-made automobile, you first have to be trained. In addition to being trained to push the right button at the right time, you are trained in the intricacies of human relationships. Under high-sounding names such as communication skills, interpersonal skills, adapting skills, or sales techniques, you are trained in how to look someone in the eye, how to smile, how to sit, how to cross your legs, how to stand, how to fold your arms, how to walk, how to comb your hair, and how to scratch when no one is looking. Let me emphasize that. You are trained in all those behaviors. But so is my dog when he learns not to go to the bathroom on the carpet.

In the midst of all this training, do you ever wonder if there may be something a little deeper than this?

In the course of my work, I visit a high-powered executive regularly. This man rose to a position of importance despite the fact that he really doesn't have a lot of personality.

So his company sent him to all the seminars, and now he has been trained. When I go into his office, he comes from behind his desk and sits in the chair next to me. He unfolds his arms, bends forward, looks me in the eye, and nods his head as I talk. And do you know what's happened in spite of all of this fine training? He's still a turkey.

Instead of having no personality at all, he has a textbook personality, and that's as phony as an Elvis imposter. That's why I would give you this T-shirt. I want you to have a constant reminder that if you don't have it, you don't accomplish much by faking it.

But that's not an easy suggestion. That's a plea for honesty, and honesty isn't always the simplest route. Sometimes we don't know what the truth is, and even when we do, it takes a lot of courage to face it.

So I offer you three suggestions. You've heard them before, but they become particularly important to you now as you stand in one spot and wonder how to get to the next one.

Know Thyself

I use that old word form on purpose because I want this to sound intellectual. And it is. It was first uttered by one of those Greek guys, maybe Plato, and he was supposed to have been quoting from somebody named the Oracle at Delphi. This is old wisdom (often the best kind) because it has been around for 2,500 years. All of a sudden, when you go through some little event in your life like high-school graduation, old wisdom becomes amazingly modern and relevant.

During high school, you really don't have to spend a lot of time trying to know yourself. There is always someone willing to help you with the task. When I was a student, my teachers were always assisting me. They would clarify the meaning of my existence with such statements as, "Young man, I'm going to tell you what's wrong with you. You're just lazy and insensitive and immature. . . ." (As you know from senior writing class, these dots indicate that the list goes on. I would include the rest of the descriptions, but I never listened past that point. Three adjectives in a row are about as much as I can handle.)

When our teachers weren't helping us identify ourselves, friends and parents were willing to offer some assistance. I always found big brothers and sisters to be particularly capable help.

After you get all this information about who you are from a wide variety of sources, you sit down and take those tests that not only describe you but give you numbers to prove the point.

Finally, you get to see the counselor. This is the one person who really knows you, forward and backward, inside out, upside down. This person knows you better than you can ever know yourself because he has the proof. He has the test scores.

When that big moment comes, the counselor moves from behind the desk, looks at your tests, and says, "Now let me see here, according to your test results, you really ought to become, well, let's look at this, a brain surgeon? No, that's not right. No, according to the scores, you would be perfectly equipped to be a horse trainer."

You are the only person in the world who knows that you are allergic to fly bites. Regardless of what the tests show, regardless of all the good advice you have received through the years, you're the only one who really knows this pertinent piece of information, and you know that nobody who is allergic to fly bites could ever be successful as a horse trainer.

At this moment you realize that if you are going to make it in life, you alone will have to make an honest assessment of yourself because you know yourself better than anyone else does.

This challenge is so astounding that it probably makes you want to take another test. Since you have already had tests that are graded, I have designed another little test for you that doesn't use any grades. It doesn't even require that you have two number-two pencils, nor do you need a pin to punch holes in your answer sheet. All you need for my test is a little fishing time and your own honesty. Are you ready for the first question?

Question 1: Do You Love God?

Don't quote me Bible verses and don't show me your Sunday school perfect attendance medal. I want an honest answer. I am not interested in the language of love. I want to know if you love God, if within your heart there is a burning desire to please God, to make Him happy with the kind of things you do and the kind of thoughts you think.

Knowing this is the beginning to knowing yourself. If you can answer this question honestly, you will always have some idea about how you relate to people, how you work at your job, and what you will and will not do when temptation comes. The refreshing reality is that you are the only person in the world who can answer this question. Other people can see your actions and make some guesses, but you are the only one who can really know for sure.

Question 2: Are You a Good Friend?

If you have to ask what I mean by "good," score yourself a "no" on this question. You should know the answer without needing any clarification. But a deeper level is implied here.

The real question is twofold: Are you capable of loving another person, and are you capable of receiving love? Don't shout out the answer until you have gone fishing on it. Being able to accept another person's love is often one of the hardest fights and sweetest victories of our lives.

Question 3: Are You Capable of Doing Your Best?

Sure, it would make an easier test if I would specify what area I'm asking about—jobs, sports, music, playing. But my question is more general and more difficult than that. Are you capable of doing your best in anything you try? Obviously, you will never do your best in everything, but can you do it in some areas?

To say yes says a lot about yourself. It says that you really do know what your best is. That's good, because many of us don't know. We sometimes get snared in two traps. We might convince ourselves to accept less than our best so that we are always working at about half speed when we really think we are giving it our all. On the other hand, we might tell ourselves that our best is really more than we can do and we spend our lives feeling guilty and depressed. Either way, we have not been honest.

To know what your best is—and to know that you are capable of doing it in at least one arena of your life—tells you a great deal about yourself. If you master that, you've passed the test, and you are ready for the second suggestion.

Be Yourself

Do you remember when you were in the fourth grade and you went through that period when you thought no one liked you? You were so despondent that you asked your mother how to make friends. Your mother smiled, hugged you, brushed away your tears, and spoke profoundly. "Just be yourself, dear. Don't try to impress people with what you're not. Just act natural." At that moment in your life, you didn't understand that advice at all.

You *were* being yourself, and that was the problem. You really wanted to be that other kid in the fourth grade who had all the friends.

Again, when you were a sophomore and earned your first date, you went back to consult the Oracle of Mom. "How am I supposed to act on a date?" you asked, trying to hide the fact that you were scared to death.

Again, your mother smiled, hugged you, and spoke profoundly. "Just be yourself, dear. Just be yourself. Don't try to impress people with what you're not. Just act natural."

Again you didn't understand that advice at all. You really wanted to be that other sophomore kid who seemed to have years of dating experience and had mastered the technique of cool.

As always, mother's advice is the best, whether you are in fourth grade or a sophomore or forty years old. The best way to handle any situation is just to be yourself.

That's a hard lesson to learn because you have to remind yourself constantly.

But once you learn it, it solves a bunch of problems. If you can learn to be yourself, you don't need as good a memory. When you are busy putting on airs, trying to impress, you have to clutter your mind with a lot to think about it. It's easier to learn to be yourself.

Give Yourself

If you are having trouble talking with people (or as the experts say, with interpersonal communications), you can go to a seminar and learn to look people in the eye. You can learn the skill, but the problem is still there, the reason why you couldn't look someone in the eye in the first place.

At this point you need to examine your heart. I'm not even

going to ask whether you like people or don't like people or whether you're shy or bold. Those are cop-out questions. What I am going to ask is whether you are willing to give yourself.

Christ left the joy of heaven to come to earth to teach us this. Once here, He died on the cross and gave the lesson even more emphasis. While He was here, He taught us the creed for it. He said, "Love your neighbor as yourself" (Matt. 19:19).

We could turn this into a theological discussion and throw in a lot of Greek, or we could make a claim about the need to love yourself first and how you go about achieving that. But we can learn a simple lesson here without the clutter.

When you encounter someone else, you need to give that person as much attention as you give yourself. The whole practice of social manners is based on this principle. It's just a matter of considering how you would feel if you were the person watching you.

By the same reasoning, when you do a job, you need to do it as if you were the person who benefits from that job. In other words, you need to give yourself in every facet of your life. Now that implies that you have whipped the "I" problem. You know the one: "I know what I want"; "I know what I need"; "I . . . I . . . I."

This is our path to happiness—knowing ourselves, accepting ourselves, and giving ourselves.

That's the message you wear on your T-shirt, and it is one worth telling.

I need to tell you a tragic story. I warn you before you go on; if you don't enjoy unhappy endings, you may want to skip this.

This story is about a fellow who went to high school. He wasn't a particularly great student nor did he have a sparkling personality. But he was a solid basketball player, and the team was good that year.

Our tragic hero played well, achieved some distinction, and basked in the glory. When he came on the court, people cheered. When he scored, the band played a little refrain. After the game, students and teachers came up and praised him. One rather pretty cheerleader took a special interest in him. (Well, maybe she wasn't interested in him, but she was interested in all that success.)

Eventually, the fellow suffered a transition—he graduated. He went off to college with dreams of being a basketball star there, but things didn't work out that way. The other people at college were as good as he was, if not better. No one cheered him, no band played, no teachers praised him, and no cheerleader paid heed to his success.

Drained of his glory, he came home after the first semester, and now he hangs around doing odd jobs, not going anywhere in particular. But he still plays basketball. He plays in the get-up games out at the park. He plays in church league, although he goes to church only to qualify; and he hangs around the high-school games remembering the good old days when he was great.

I warned you that this was a tragic story, and it's tragic for one reason. This fellow never learned the lesson of your T-shirt. Yesterday is history.

At this point in your life, you need to come to grips with this. As depressing as it may sound, high school is over. That phase of your life has concluded, and you can't ever do it again. Yesterday is history.

You are probably screaming by now, "You don't need to tell me that. I'm so glad it's over that you will never catch me looking back, not ever in my weakest moments. No, sir, I'm through."

Well, I'm pleased to see you so firm; I just hope you stay that way. But I want to remind you that there will always be that temptation to live in the past. It can attack about anytime. Just because you survive the first few weeks or months after high school doesn't mean you are safe. This feeling of wanting to live in history attacks people of every age.

Regardless of where we are in our lives or what we are doing, there are always three directions to look. We could spend our time, our energies, and our dreams looking into the future. That seems to be the best direction because that is the direction in which we are going. But looking into the future can be scary, since we really don't know what's out there.

Wouldn't life be a lot simpler if we could at least have some hint? But most of the time we don't even have that much. About the only scope we can use to look into the future is our imaginations, and those can get carried away, particularly if we have just overdosed on some fantasy movie. There is no way we can get a clear insight into what the future holds.

The next direction we can look toward is the present, but that is often tedious. The present is demanding and depressing, and it always seems to require rat chasing. We tell ourselves that we need to get up at 5:00 A.M. tomorrow. We have to run here. We have to run there. We get yelled at for being late. We have no friends. We have no glory. Based on what is happening now, we have no promise in the future.

When we get to this point, we really have to avoid the temptation of looking toward the past. We look at the past through our memories, which are often quite selective. If we are not careful, we remember only the good times. Somehow we begin to remember high school as a time when we were secure and less harried, and we wish we were back there. This is when we forget that yesterday is history.

It's all right to remember, even healthy at times. That's why people attend class reunions; they want to remember a bit. But we can't waste our days and our lives wishing we could reclaim that glory. When we do that, we don't take charge of the direction we are going—into the future.

Before you dismiss this piece of T-shirt wisdom as something from Mr. Green Jeans on "Captain Kangaroo," let me remind you that it's from the Bible. Jesus said, "No one, having put his hand to the plow, and looking back, is fit for the kingdom of God" (Luke 9:62).

In other words, as anybody who has ever been on a farm will tell you, if you want to move forward in a straight line, you have to fix your sight on some definite object in front of you.

By now you may have figured out that this T-shirt is about setting goals. Setting goals, in simple terms, is the process of clarifying the future.

There are periods in our lives, such as high-school days, when setting goals doesn't seem to be a really urgent matter. That is more or less taken care of in day-by-day living. Oh, there are some little short-term goals such as deciding when to get up tomorrow and when to finish the paper that is due in history class, but those long-term far-reaching goals that make the head hurt from peering so far into the future just aren't necessary.

But one day, we run headfirst into a major transition called high-school graduation, and we suddenly find ourselves facing the enormous task of trying to find a place in the future that we need to plow toward to keep the furrow straight.

Congratulations on getting to this point in your life. I do hope you are enjoying it. Not everyone does; some people find these goal-setting times to be frustrating.

To master the art of setting goals and escape some of that frustration, you need to consider two points: (1) where you are now and how you got here, and (2) where you want to be. Let's look at both a bit more closely.

1. Where you are now and how you got here. We consider this point first because it takes the fear out of examining the second point.

Not long ago I attended a conference for high-school teachers. The speaker challenged the audience: "Are you preparing those young students to live their futures?" Some teachers allowed that little thought to throw them into a state of guilt. Others simply dismissed it as an unreasonable request. They argued, "How can we prepare anyone for the future when we have no idea what the future is going to be?"

But the problem isn't really as tough as either group makes it out to be. We may not know what the future is going to be, but we do know who's going to live in it—you are. And we prepare for the future by analyzing how we live in the present. To understand this, let's look at two points of reality.

• God has been faithful to you up to now. You have to admit that. You haven't achieved what you have without God's help. At every step, you had His companionship. Now consider the second point of reality.

• Chances are 100 percent that God is going to be faithful

to you in the future. In the days to come, you just have to remember how you got to where you are now. Regardless of what you decide to do, regardless of how situations develop, God will be faithful to you. That's the promise of the future.

2. *Where do you want to be?* Now that you realize how you got where you are, it's time for you to pick a spot in front of you where you would really like to be.

Probably your first reaction to this task is dread. It sounds so tedious and boring. Nevertheless, you need to analyze yourself with some kind of objective measuring stick. You need to accept your strengths and weaknesses.

Based on this analysis, you need to be reasonable, rational, and sensible in setting goals for the future. Some inspirational speakers even suggest that you go so far as to draw a time line around the walls of your room and move patches along the time line showing your progress. Others recommend that you write yourself notes to be read ten, fifteen, or fifty years from now.

But while you are doing all this, you really need to be objective and reasonable. We old-timers love to accuse you younger people of being silly. And the word we use to describe your silliness is *idealistic*. You've heard us. We've probably already spoken to you about it.

"Ha. Ha. Your plans are charming but unrealistic. Someday soon, my dear, reality will set in and you won't be so, well, so idealistic."

Balderdash! (Do you like that word? I was going to say "Fiddlesticks" but balderdash seems to be more communicative.) Balderdash! Now's the time to dream. Yes, that's what I said. This time of goal setting is a time to dream big, to let your mind run free and see yourself in your dreams ten, fifteen, or fifty years from now. Don't draw fences around yourself. Dream.

Of course, before you run completely wild, we both need to remind ourselves that there are two kinds of dreams: foolish dreams and dreams of reality.

Foolish dreams are those few that deny God's work in your life. If you are five feet six inches tall, not particularly quick, and not blessed with unusual hand and eye coordination, it would probably be foolish for you to dream about playing in the NBA.

Dreams of reality become the landmark that we plow toward to keep the furrow straight. But these dreams are more than that; they are the devices we use to lift the limits imposed by our own minds. Most of us are capable of more than what we are doing. You've already been told that. Frequently, your high-school teachers reminded you, "You're just not working up to your potential." You are probably sick of hearing people say it, but I am still going to say it again. Most of our limits are only in our minds.

Let me illustrate that point with something from the world of sports. Several years ago, I coached high-school track. One season, I had a tall, strong runner who participated in the 440-yard run. (Notice that I am a prehistoric beast. I coached way back in the ancient days when we ran yards instead of meters.) Not only was this fellow tall and strong, but he liked to win. And that's a good combination. His top speed, the very best that he could do, was good enough to win his races during the early part of the season. He could run the distance in fifty-three seconds, and he could beat the competition.

We worked hard in practice for months trying to get him beyond fifty-three seconds, but he just couldn't make it. He had hit the maximum of his potential. That was the best he could ever do.

But one day in a track meet, this fellow with that "natural" limitation had to run his race in fifty seconds to beat the competition. He did it. Did you hear that? He ran his race a full three seconds faster than what he had been capable of running. After that, he always ran fifty seconds.

Here's an example that involves the whole human race. For years, the best of the whole human race ran a distance of one mile in four minutes in track competition. For years and years, no one could cover the distance faster than that. Most experts agreed that it was humanly impossible to run that distance any faster. But one day in 1955 somebody beat that four-minute limitation, and now a multitude of people are faster than the human limit used to be.

That's the work of dreams: to lift the limits of our minds and let us see clearly the spot in the future that pulls us forward and directs us along the way.

I have had frequent opportunities to talk with fifty-, sixty-, and seventy-year-old people who were being honored for mastering great accomplishments in life. They had written great books, made significant contributions, or endured hardships to master some feat. The question I always ask is, "Did you ever think that you would accomplish what you have accomplished?"

The answer is always the same. With the look of pleasant memories in their eyes, they say, "Well, when I was young, I dreamed about it."

That's what keeps us plowing straight.

ARE WE THERE
YET?

As long as you stay in school, at any level, you will always have an attainable goal in front of you—to finish school. Every day you will always know exactly where you are going. Your activities lead somehow to that goal.

Another good thing about a goal like that is that you measure how far you have come and how much you have left. The goal of finishing school gives you direction and reminds you that you are making progress.

Regardless of whether you want to admit it or not, you have learned to depend on that goal. It has provided you with security through the years.

But what happens when you finish school? What's the next goal? What is going to give you direction and let you mark progress?

This question is often overwhelming to high-school and college graduates alike. I have thousands of examples, enough examples to give me reason to tell you that this is one of the major hurdles that you will face in your life. This is the challenge of the whole transition—setting a new long-range goal.

The reason for the dilemma is obvious. Finishing school is such an all-consuming activity that we really don't have time to determine the goal following that. Then when we accomplish our goal by graduating, we don't know where we are going.

At this point you need to realize the character of a goal. There is a difference between a goal and a life-style. Some graduates tell me that their next goal is to have a comfortable life, a good job, and someone to share it with. But that isn't a goal. That doesn't give you direction and help you determine progress. You are going to need something a bit more definite.

One alternative might be to set some temporary goals. Some people manage with these; some people even manage with rather frivolous temporary goals. For example, I am a jogger. A goal in my life, one objective in my mind every day, is to run 1,500 miles this year.

"How frivolous," you say. "How utterly silly."

Maybe so, but at least I have a goal.

Every night before I go to sleep when I take inventory of myself, I know whether I have moved toward my goal that day. I know how far I have come and how far I have left to go.

As I spend day after day chasing rats, I at least have some sense of which direction is forward.

I'd like to offer you a suggestion. If you find yourself running around aimlessly after finishing school, you may want to consider the virtue of some definite, achievable short-term goals to help you determine if you are still moving and which direction is forward.

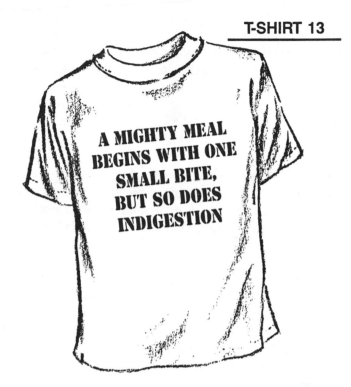

A MIGHTY MEAL
BEGINS WITH ONE
SMALL BITE,
BUT SO DOES
INDIGESTION

Setting goals is an important topic for you during this transition period of high-school graduation. There are several techniques for making some bit of information stand out and take on importance. I could do what your teachers did and write this on the board. As any student will tell you, if the teacher writes it on the board, it's important. Of course, if the teacher writes it on the board and then stands in front of it while he explains it to you, it's even more important.

On the other hand, I could give you a daily quiz until you mastered it, put it on colored paper, or repeat myself about four billion times. But I won't do that. Instead I will present you with another T-shirt, and you can wear the message on your chest for an extra day.

This shirt doesn't say anything new, but it does remind you

of an obvious point that you shouldn't forget: We need to take small steps en route to our long-term goal. We could call those short-term goals, or we might say that we need to chop up our life's plan into bite-sized chunks. Since I like to eat, that's the image we will use.

These bite-sized chunks serve three functions. First, they are logical steps we must take to achieve our dreams of reality. There are lots of illustrations of how this works, and one of the best is in the area of learning.

Once I wanted to learn to juggle. I thought that it would be fun to do and might even help me release some tension. I tried to learn by watching people do it, but it was too complicated. I couldn't tell what the jugglers were doing, and when I tried to copy what I thought I saw, I hit myself in the head with the ball I was using.

Then one day, I bumped into a girl sitting outside her classroom in the hall of her high school. She was juggling. I asked her if she would show me how. She said, "Sure. Make your left hand do this." So I did. And then she said, "Make your right hand do this." I did that and started juggling. I learned to juggle by breaking the technique into bite-sized chunks.

That's what we need to do in every phase of our lives. As I told you, this isn't a new idea. You may have even read it on T-shirts in such gems as, "Today is the first day of the rest of your life"; "A thousand mile trip starts with a single step"; "The hardest part of the job is beginning"; and "If you want to write a book, you have to write the first sentence." Or as my dad used to say, "If you want ice cream, you have to milk a cow."

If we've heard this a thousand times, why does it take so long to learn it? The world is filled with people your age who see their goals so clearly that they want to skip the steps it takes to get there. In fact, that's one criticism the older generation has of your generation. No one wants to start at the bottom, but somebody has to.

I have a friend who owns an office-cleaning business. He

hires people to clean offices at the end of the workday. He has several levels of employees—cleaners, supervisors, inspectors, consultants, and vice presidents.

Because this business is growing and needs workers, it offers ample opportunity for rapid advancement. The problem is that you can't advance until you prove yourself as a cleaner, and he can't find people who are willing to do that. He has several applicants for inspectors, consultants, and vice presidents, but not many for cleaners. You could have a perfectly realistic dream to be a vice president in this company, and you could achieve it fairly soon. That is, if you're willing to take the first step and clean offices.

When I was in junior high school, I dreamed of being a major league baseball player. I know that dream bordered on being foolish; nevertheless, that was my dream. But I made a serious mistake. I forgot to get in shape before tryouts and didn't even make the high-school team. Do you get my message? My desire to become a major league baseball player was a rather ambitious dream, but the first step was a simple matter of doing some running and lifting some weights. I didn't even survive that.

Now take a look at what you have aspired to be. What is the first chunk you need to bite off to get there? If you can answer that question, you now have a goal.

The second function of these bite-sized chunks is that they serve as motivators. Again I refer to a farm illustration, the carrot on the stick. Supposedly, a farmer would motivate a balky mule by tying a carrot on a stick and holding it in front of the mule as he plodded along. To make a straight furrow, the farmer needed to fix his gaze at the end of the row. But it wouldn't do much good to put that carrot down there. The mule couldn't see it, and he wouldn't be motivated to pull the plow that far just for the carrot. Thus, the farmer put the carrot up close on the end of a stick.

This is the way these bite-sized chunks work. On those days when the long-range goal seems a million years away and on the other side of the world, we can at least find some satisfaction in achieving the little steps that get us there.

The third function of the bite-sized chunks is that they serve as finishing spots, and we need those regularly. You learned this lesson during your high-school days. There is no feeling quite as fulfilling as finishing the school year. Do you remember how you felt? You cleaned out your locker, threw away old papers, turned in those old textbooks, and breathed. It was wonderful, the feeling of accomplishment and the sense that it was over.

Now, if you have a career dream thirty years into the future, you need to build in some finishing spots along the way. You can't wait another thirty years to feel the way you do when you finish a school term. You need those spots on more regular occasions.

You also need to understand that some professions have very few of those spots built into the nature of the work. Since I am a teacher and know that profession best, I will use it for an illustration. Since I deal with real people, there aren't many times that I can stand at the end of the assembly line and say, "Look, I made that. Look how nicely the doors fit and how smoothly the paint flowed on. I finished that, and I am proud of what I've done. Now it's time to build another one."

Nope. Teaching doesn't provide many of these moments. So as a teacher, I take the same joy in the end of the semester as you do. The end of the semester is not my thirty-year goal, but it is one step. Finishing a semester gives me some real joy and starts me on the next bite-sized chunk.

Now that you have dreamed your big dreams and set some short-term goals along the way, don't overlook the value of bite-sized chunks.

THE FACE OF
SUCCESS

What do you think about success? Notice how I phrased that. I did it on purpose. The intent of this T-shirt is not for me to lecture you on success, but to find out what you think about it. It's a question we all have to answer for ourselves.

I could give you my definition of success. It wouldn't do you much good, though, because it's my definition and won't fit you. Success is like a shoe; everybody has to find an individual fit.

Not having your own definition of success is so risky to your mental health that it probably deserves a warning from the surgeon general. If you try to wander through life without your own definition of success, you will always walk in a cloud of unhappiness.

To find your own definition, let's look at some people and see if we can label them successful or unsuccessful.

Today's newspaper carried a tragic story. A very "successful" high-school student, one who had good grades, friends, a bright future, just took his own life. When the reporter called this student "successful," what definition was she using, and would you be willing to use the same one for yourself?

Is Mother Teresa a success? Oh sure, you say she is now, but that's because the outside world discovered her and made her famous. But if she had worked in obscurity all her life without all that attention, would you have called her life a success?

I have a friend who is an insurance salesman, and he is good! He is highly respected among his clients and the people in the field. He is one of the top salesmen in the nation, and he makes lots of money. He has a new home, new cars, and a place of importance in the community. Would you call him successful?

Would you change your mind if I told you that his family is falling apart while he continues to be important in the field and make lots of money?

Would it make a difference if I told you that this man really doesn't want to be an insurance salesman? He really doesn't enjoy the work all that much. He dreams about teaching high-school history and coaching basketball. With his personality and enthusiasm, he would probably be good at those jobs. I am sure his students would learn, and he would win lots of games.

But he isn't a teacher and a coach because those professions don't pay enough money. So this man gets up every morning, goes into the insurance world, and spends his day chasing rats while he dreams of being a basketball coach. Do you think he is successful?

Is a mother who spends her life cooking meals, cleaning house, refereeing fights, and running the family limo service a success?

Those examples should help you start thinking; at least you

should see the problem. How are you going to define success in your life, and how will you know that you are within the boundaries of your own definition?

If you don't work through this, you may have a couple of problems. The first possibility is that without your own definition, you will always let someone else define success for you. And there are always people who would like to do that. Several years ago I taught in a high school where a very bright young man was a student. He was the leader in nearly every class he took, always at the top, always setting the curve. Don't you hate people like that? During his senior year, he took the ACT test, and as expected, he scored very high. College recruiters camped on his doorstep. All the people in town cheered for this young man.

But when this fellow finished high school, he didn't go to college. He took over his father's gas station. He runs it still, and he is good at running it. But I don't think the town has ever forgiven him. Every time I visit, somebody mentions this man and says with a sigh, "He could have been such a success."

But shouldn't we argue that he is a success because he found the courage to define success himself rather than letting someone else do it for him?

The other problem of not having your own definition is that you might fall into the trap of using numbers to define success. If a coach wins 50 percent of her games, is she successful, or must she win 80 percent? If you earn x dollars, are you successful, or must you earn twice as much? Can you be a successful student with a grade of 80 percent, or must you make a 90 percent to meet the standard?

Of course, you could argue that it all depends on the person involved. That is exactly my point. To avoid the pitfalls, you must develop your own definition of success.

Let me help you get started. But first let me remind you that success covers a broader area than just career. It also includes your life as a spouse, as a parent, as a person, and as a child of

God. At any rate, your definition of success should meet three requirements.

1. Your definition of success should recognize your God-given talents. God gave you specific gifts and put you here to use those gifts so this world would be a better place. Whatever you decide to do and whatever you decide is success must recognize God-given talent and purpose. To define success in less than this is to cheat God.

2. Your definition of success should challenge you to work to your potential. I realize that this may sound like the first requirement, but it is so important that I want to state it both ways. The young man in the service station is a success because the task gives him the opportunity to use his ability. He isn't cheating his gifts; he is just using them in the position of his choice.

You already know the value of this requirement. You know that you aren't satisfied when you are not giving your best. If you use a standard of success that's beneath your ability, you will always be dissatisfied with what you have accomplished.

3. Your definition of success should bring you personal joy. Let me say that another way: The result of success is happiness. Since only you know for sure what makes you happy, only you can know what success is.

Once you know that, you can wear a smile. Then the world will know, too.

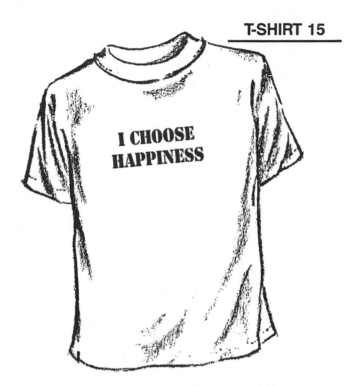

I CHOOSE HAPPINESS

Perhaps we ought to discuss the nature of happiness. I've made an extensive study of happy and unhappy people through my life, though I admit that most of my research has been unintentional. I just run into people who fall into one category or the other. Nearly everybody I meet is either happy or unhappy, so I'm always gathering evidence.

Sometimes I meet people who have every right to be happy, and they are. Sometimes I meet people who have every right to be unhappy, and they are. On the other hand, often I meet people who have the right to be happy but aren't, and vice versa. My conclusion is that happiness isn't a scientific phenomenon. It isn't predictable, so there is obviously an unexplainable variable at work. In my attempt to explain that variable in something catchy enough to put on the front of the

T-shirt, I am happy to report: Happiness is a state of mind.

To accept that little piece of truth is to buy yourself some freedom. You don't have to waste time wishing you were somewhere else.

Most of us spend our lives telling ourselves that happiness is around the corner. When you were in high school, you dreamed of a happier time when you would get out. Now that you are out of high school, you dream of a happier time when you were back in. When you are working, you dream of happiness at a party this Friday night. When you are on the lowest rung of your career ladder, you dream of the happy times when you become a vice president.

It is a vicious circle, this dreaming of happier times and places. There is no such thing as a happy or an unhappy school. There is no such thing as a happy or an unhappy party. There is no such thing as a happy or an unhappy job. The quality of happiness or unhappiness is determined by you and not by the situation. Happiness is *your* choice.

This really shouldn't come as any great surprise; the Bible is filled with all sorts of reminders. Jesus speaks of the abundant life; Peter talks of a joy unspeakable; Paul refers to peace beyond understanding. In Romans 8:28 Paul puts this promise of peace in perspective when he says, "And we know that all things work together for good to those who love God, to those who are the called according to His purpose."

I have met many happy people who confirm this for me. A few years ago I became acquainted with a woman who was dying of cancer. In the few months I knew her, she had several surgeries and was in constant pain. Yet she remained one of the happiest people I have ever met. When I was having a bad day, I would find myself going to visit this terminally ill woman so that she could cheer me up. She taught me the lesson: Regardless of how desperate the situation, you can choose to be happy.

You must always remember that it is your choice.

Perhaps you have experienced this shirt's message in your dating life. Do you remember that time you really wanted to go out with a particular person? You flirted and made eyes, wrote names in your notebook, and whispered secrets to your friends. Do you remember how fun and exciting this was? Then one day the big event happened. If you are a guy, you got up the courage to ask her out. If you are a girl, you got up the courage to make him ask. And the date was arranged.

More excitement set in. You asked to use the family car, got a new hairdo, tried on your clothes in front of a mirror, practiced making date talk, and you might even have kissed the back of your hand to see if the mouth knew how to function should the need arise. Do you remember how much fun this was?

Finally, the day of the date arrived, and you went out with that very special person. And it was only so-so. That's when you learned the truth—often the fun is in getting and not necessarily in having.

This is true in many situations. You will dream of the fun of having a college degree. But if getting the degree isn't much fun, having one won't be much fun, either. You will dream of having an important job, but if getting the job isn't much fun, having the job probably won't be, either.

Have you ever watched a television program where someone is being honored for a great accomplishment? Have you ever noticed that often the honoree looks rather bored with the whole ordeal? And you say to yourself, "Is that an ungrateful person or what?" Probably this person isn't ungrateful; he or she just knows that the fun was getting to the accomplishment rather than being honored for it.

The problem with dreaming of some honor is that we deceive ourselves by thinking that the honor will change us, when it really doesn't. The process of getting to the honor may change us, but the honor itself doesn't.

Let's make a list of some of the great privileges of life.
1. Taking cuts in the lunch line.
2. Having a locker near the English classroom.
3. Choosing a restaurant when the family eats out.
4. Staying out past curfew on special nights.
5. Working.

Whoops! How did that last one get in there? We were listing privileges, so why is work included?

That's the purpose of this shirt, to convince ourselves that work really is a great privilege. At first glance, that idea might come as a surprise. Haven't we always believed that work was a necessary evil, a torture we had to endure to provide for our basic needs? How can work be one of life's privileges? Let's ponder that for a moment.

I think it was Mark Twain who said, "If there isn't any work in heaven, I don't want to go there." (Of course, when he said that, Twain wasn't really committed on the idea of going to heaven at all.)

Privilege depends on choice. We can choose work as a privilege, or we can view it in negative terms.

You have already had some experience with this. You have probably held a job, and you have surely had the responsibility of family chores at one time or another. These count as work. Now you have to ask yourself whether you have discovered the true meaning of the privilege yet.

If you haven't, you need to work on it. While you are in school, you are leading a life of preparation. Even if you do have a job or endless chores, you are still in the role of preparation.

Once you have finished school, that role changes to performance. Now is the time for you to apply your preparation to some endeavor you choose. In other words, it's time to go to work.

If you are one of the fortunate persons in this country, you will spend about one-fourth of the rest of your life at work. (Before you get depressed about that, remember that you will spend more time than that asleep, so it averages out.) Since you're going to spend so much of your life working, you need to consider your attitude toward the privilege of getting a job and fulfilling its demands.

One of the privileges of work is making money. However, if making money becomes your only goal or motivation, you have a problem.

I have seen a bumper sticker with a rather sad message: "I owe, I owe, so it's off to work I go." Now isn't that sad? This short message tells a lot about the driver. This person may find some joy in possession, because he has evidently gone into debt to possess something. But other than that, there doesn't seem to be any joy in that one-fourth of his life we call work.

The most obvious suggestion for him is to change jobs, but

changing jobs isn't always that easy. A simpler suggestion, but one that may be more difficult to implement, is for him to change his attitude. Let's put that in catchy wording suitable for a T-shirt: "If you can't change jobs, change attitudes."

What do you think? Will this guy buy it?

Work affords privileges beyond just making money. For example, work gives us the privilege of contributing something to our employers, to our communities, and even to the world. This privilege of feeling that we have contributed is vital to your well-being.

I frequently have the opportunity to talk to high-school students who are pondering the possibility of dropping out of school. Usually, their main reason for wanting to drop out is that they want to feel they are making a contribution. You sometimes have to be alert to hear them say it, but it's there.

"I want to drop out of school," they tell me, as if their minds are made up and won't be changed.

"Why?"

"Because I have to make some money," they tell me.

"But you seem to have money. Your parents must give you as much as you need."

"But you don't understand," they say. "I don't want the money they give me. I want the money I make." In other words, "I need to feel that I am making a contribution."

I sometimes see the same need at the other end of the age spectrum. People who complained about having to work finally reach retirement age. You would think that they would be happy about it, but often they aren't. If they don't find some other way to feel they are making a contribution, those people can become unhappy and sick, both physically and mentally.

When we make a contribution through our work, we also accomplish other purposes. We explore the limits of our abilities; we use our creative talents; and we contribute to the beauty and joy of this world. In short, we learn at least one way of fulfilling the purpose of life itself. We learn how to use our time, our efforts, and our abilities to glorify God with our very existence. Those factors help us to find the right attitude toward our work.

Now, let's take a look at how this attitude works in daily living. Let's suppose for a minute that you have found some backbreaking, menial job in a local sweatbox. In other words, let's assume that you have just gone to work at a fast-food joint. (That's a fair assumption, given that about one-fifth of the work force begin their careers at fast-food joints.)

Your first question is to ask for whom you actually work. You may as well ask it because you are going to have to answer to everyone you meet anyway. That's the second question of the Catechism of Polite Conversation.

Surely you know the ritual by now. When you meet people you hardly know, in the store or on the street or even at church, the first question is always, "How are you?" And the second question is, "Well, what are you doing these days?"

In recent years the social critics, those people who stay up late at night to worry about what is wrong with America, have told us that this line of questioning in the Catechism of Polite Conversation is actually arrogant and rude; it is typically American because just asking indicates the emphasis we put on work. (As you remember from ninth-grade civics, that emphasis in our country is called the work ethic, or maybe even the Puritan ethic.)

Since I have decided never to argue with social critics, I don't know whether the question is rude or not, but I do agree with part of what they say. I do agree that the people asking it really are asking something more significant and profound than just, "Who's paying you?" I think the question implies deeper meaning: "What are you doing to satisfy your need to make a contribution and to realize your potential and worth?" It's all in the question.

That's why your answer will probably never be totally satisfactory to you. The easiest way to answer the question, cut short the casual meeting, and get out of the rest of the interrogation is simply to name the chain of fast-food joint. Immediately, your questioner will be able to discern such details as to whether you spend your time frying beef or chicken, whether the fries come in straight lines or little curls, and who sings the commercial—important details all.

Besides that, your answer is correct. You do work for the chain, and that little thought should be stuck in the back of your mind every moment you wear the uniform. Regardless of how much money the company spends on advertising and who sings the commercials, your face, or your voice, is the one that most customers identify with the chain. In short, you are the chain.

When people speak of the friendliness or cleanliness or even efficiency of the chain, they are actually speaking of you. That's rather a scary thought, isn't it? But you need to know that. That's how it is in the world of production.

Yet as you answer your questioner with the name of the chain, you realize that the answer is a bit inaccurate. You also work for the local person who is either the owner or the manager of that particular store. That's the person who writes your check, decides on your raise, and picks your days off.

Again, remembering your ninth-grade civics class, you know enough about business to know that if that person makes money, you might even make more money. If that person is happy, you might even be happier. If you have a good attitude about work, your attitude might even help that person have a better attitude. In effect, you work for a particular person instead of some giant conglomerate operated by faceless bureaucrats with briefcases.

But in a deeper sense, you work for yourself. Your purpose in working is not necessarily to make the chain a fortune so it can buy advertising spots during the Super Bowl. Your purpose in working is not necessarily to make the local person more money, which in turn produces some joy in his heart and smiles on his face. Actually, your purpose in working is to fulfill your need to feel that you are making a contribution. Your purpose in working is to use your ability and time to do something significant and in so doing glorify God.

I have often heard people complain that their particular work is beneath their dignity, and it's easy to fall into that trap. It's easy to get caught up in looking where we are not—to say something like, "Well, here I am wasting my time boxing burgers when I know I have the talent to move up to the french fry machine." It's good to aspire, but at the same time, it's necessary to remember that there is no inherent dignity in any job. The dignity comes from the person doing the job. Any job has dignity when you approach it with the right attitude.

And when you go to work with the right attitude, good things happen. The chain gets rich, and it in turn enriches our lives by providing us with cute commercials and enchanting jingles. The local owner gets rich, and he smiles a lot and sponsors a Little League team. But you are the real winner. You get to feel that you have done your best and have done something significant. You get to feel like a poet who has just written his inspired masterpiece.

When you finally achieve this attitude, you are ready to celebrate one of life's great privileges—the right to work.

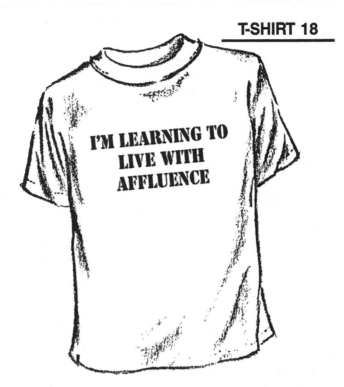

To live a really happy life and to discover the true joy of success, you have to understand the concept of money. Specifically, you have to come to grips with the meaning of a quantity of money called "enough." Enough is an elusive quantity. You can't hold it in your hand, you can't count it, and you can't weigh it. Enough never means the same to two people, and it never means the same to one person throughout life.

One day not long ago, you sat in British lit class and dreamed of the future when you could get a real job and make money. At that time, you probably dreamed of a specific amount of money, and to you, that was the accepted quantity of enough. But notice how that quantity has changed now that you are out of school, particularly if you have a job paying you what you once thought was enough.

– 81 –

For most of us, that's the way it works throughout our lives. We dream of enough, but when we get there, we suddenly realize that enough is not really enough anymore.

In fact, to define the quantity of enough, we have to come to grips with another quantity called "not quite." It works this way.

"Does your new job pay enough?" someone asks.

"Not quite," we answer.

"Do you have as much as you need?"

"Not quite."

"Do you have enough to buy the car you really want?"

"Not quite." And the list goes on.

Unlike enough, not quite is a definite quantity. It is the exact distance between a contented life and anxiety.

I once knew a man who enjoyed owning land. That seemed to be his biggest source of pleasure, so he worked long and hard to buy land. He always said he really didn't want all the land in the world, he wanted only the land that joined him. So he kept working and buying, but he could never quite meet his goal of owning all the land that joined him. One day, in utter despair, he died without ever having mastered the concept of the quantity of enough.

That's a money problem you are going to have to work out if you are ever going to find real happiness. We could talk about the kind of life-style you want to live and the things you want to own. We could even talk about how much you need to make and what you need to do to make that kind of money. But all that talk is worthless until you decide what is the quantity of enough.

This concept becomes important when people pick college majors and choose professions.

After we get past all the talk about service to humankind and what gives us pleasure, the honest ones will tell me that they are choosing a particular kind of work because they want to make a lot of money.

At this point, I think I am supposed to look shocked and

pious and give my sermon denouncing the temptations of worldliness and materialism. But I don't do that, and I'm not going to do it to you, either, even if you are thinking those thoughts. Instead, I am going to remind you that you need to define the quantity of enough.

If you choose a profession to make money, you had better be sure that you will make enough in that profession. If you don't know what enough is, you may never find the profession or the job that pays that much.

Not long ago, some workers in our community who make half as much as I do complained to their bosses that they were not making enough. I understand. Not long ago, some professional people in our community who make twice as much as I do complained to their bosses that they were not making enough. I think I understand. Not long ago, a famous ball player who makes $1 million per year complained to his bosses that he wasn't making enough. I don't understand.

To understand the concept of enough, we need to consider how we look at money and what function it plays in our lives. Let's examine three possibilities.

1. Some people use money to define human worth.

Some people decide who they are and what they are worth as individuals by how much they make, how much they own, or what they are capable of making and owning.

This is a simple way to approach this difficult idea of human worth, because it's easy to identify and measure. If my house is bigger than yours, I must be worth more than you are. If my savings account is bigger than yours, I must be a better person than you are. If I make more money than you do, I must be worth more to society than you are.

Now, before you protest all this and get really angry with me for bringing it up, stop and ponder all the places you see this kind of thinking. You might have even done a bit of it yourself. If you have a job that pays $3.60 per hour and your friend has a job that pays $3.90 per hour, you may catch yourself thinking, *Wait a minute, I'm worth more than that.* You can try to persuade me that the issue is really thirty cents, but that isn't true. The issue is one of human worth. You have trouble dealing with the possibility that someone is worth more money than you are. You are using money to define yourself as a person.

Notice how this has run rampant with professional athletes. If the trend continues, soon some athlete is going to have an annual salary bigger than the national debt. Do you think anybody needs that much money? Do you think that when you are making $10 million, a paltry sum like an extra $100,000 is worth all the commotion that some athlete will go through to get it? Of course it isn't. That $100,000 isn't going to change his life one iota. That $100,000 is about self-worth. It is important to the athlete to be the wealthiest player because in his mind, if he is the wealthiest, surely he is the best.

At this point, I need to ask you a tough question. Do you have any other way of defining what you are worth as a person than the money you make? If you don't, let me warn you that you may never know the meaning of enough; and like the ball player, you will always find yourself holding out for the extra paltry sum, whatever it may be.

Not long ago an insurance salesman came to help me plan my future. He took a thorough account of my assets—my house, my car, my bank account, and the pop bottles on the back porch. He put all this information into his computer and came up with a sum that was supposed to show my worth. I found the whole ordeal depressing. In his zeal for numbers, he forgot to punch in the figures that represent the worth of my wife, my children, and my granddaughter. I had to do that arithmetic myself. Since my granddaughter is worth at least $30 million, I guess that makes me the wealthiest grandfather in the world. That's the source of my human worth.

2. Some people use money for a tool.

If we define a tool as something we use to get something else, you will probably agree with this statement. Money is just a tool to get things like cars, clothes, and cassettes. Everybody understands that, and I agree. We all need things in our lives, but some people seem to need more things than other people do. Controlling that urge to use up all your money to get things is one of the difficult tasks of life. I could tell you that it is a lesson of growing up, but we both know that isn't true. We both know lots of grown-up people who haven't learned to control that urge. But it is a lesson worth learning. My experience has told me that this is the lesson of happiness and contentment.

On the other hand, some people look at money as a tool to get opportunity in the future. There are thousands of illustrations of this, but I will pick the one closest to you just now— more schooling. Sometimes people tell me that they don't plan to go to college simply because it costs too much. But does that mean they would rather use their money to get things? Some people look at the money spent on college as a way to buy opportunity somewhere down the road.

Some people look at money as a tool to get more money. That is the whole concept of investments. You are probably saying, "Yeah, I heard about that in class—how some guy got really wealthy just buying stock or real estate, but that's for rich people, not me."

Well, don't be too sure. Investing is not just a game of chance played by the rich and the famous and the readers of the *Wall Street Journal*. Regardless of what you are making just now and regardless of those urges to get things, you probably have some money left that could be used in an investment program.

If you try it for a few months, you might discover that investing is not a luxury you set aside until you get really wealthy. Investing is a habit that you learn through practice.

3. Some people look at money as a gift.

When you think about it, our money is a gift from God. After all, God gave us our ability and talent. When we use that ability and talent to make money, we must then consider that money a gift.

Thinking of our money as a gift could be one of the highlights of our lives. That idea at work in us buys us freedom and happiness.

For one thing, if we look at money as a gift, we shouldn't have too much trouble defining enough. Any sum of money should cause us to say, "Thanks, God!" The idea of money won't be our master. We won't waste a lot of creative time and energy worrying about it. We will simply agree to live with the gift we receive, and we won't envy people who seem to have a little more.

We have often heard that the Bible says money is the root of all evil, but that isn't exactly the case. The Bible says, "The love of money is a root of all kinds of evil" (1 Tim. 6:10). Looking at money as a gift should help us fight that temptation to evil in our lives.

MISTAKES ARE
STEPPING STONES

The story is told of a king who loved milk. He loved it through the day, but he particularly had to have his milk every day at exactly 4:00 P.M. Not only did he like milk, this king wanted his milk sweet and cold.

One hot summer day, the cook got busy and forgot to prepare the milk. He hadn't put it in the stream where it would stay cool, and he hadn't checked to see how sweet it was. More worried about his own head than the king's health, the cook put a little sugar in the milk, found some ice, and rolled the container over and over until he thought it would be cool enough. Then without checking, he served it to the king.

Alas, the milk had hardened from this process, and the king had to eat it with a spoon. But instead of losing his head, the cook got a place in history for inventing ice cream.

The story is told of a chemist who worked for a major corporation. He was told to develop a glue to be used for some specific product the corporation was manufacturing. But the chemist made the glue too weak; it wouldn't work for its original purpose. But instead of losing his job, the chemist got a place in history for inventing Post-it Notes. Now because of him, your teachers can scribble remarks about your paper and not even write on the copy. Or your mother can leave you notes all over the refrigerator without disturbing the enamel.

The story is told of an unemployed woman who finally took a job as a secretary. But there was one small problem; she couldn't type very well. She made so many mistakes that she was afraid of losing her job. Instead of erasing all those errors, she watered down a little white paint and started smearing that around. Instead of losing her job, she got a place in history for inventing correction fluid.

Psychologists, those people who tell the rest of us why we act strange, have said that the second biggest fear of all is the fear of failure. That's a debilitating fear. If you live in constant fear of failing, you can probably talk yourself out of trying. And not trying is a lot worse than failing. (By the way, in case you're wondering, the greatest fear is that of making a speech.)

But you have an edge on the rest of the human race. You have a T-shirt that boldly announces you aren't afraid of failure because you know the value of mistakes. In four simple words, you have a powerful, persuasive code of life.

Obviously, we don't set out to make mistakes. Those three people I told you about earlier didn't set out to make a mistake. They set out to accomplish a goal. They got sidetracked, but they made something of the diversion. They turned a mistake into a stepping stone and a stepping stone into a place in history.

The test of greatness is not that we don't make mistakes. Great people make mistakes. The test of greatness is what we do with our mistakes.

We actually have a biblical illustration for this, but we have to read it carefully. In Luke 19, Jesus tells the story of a noble-man who gave a mina to each of three servants and then left the country. When he returned, he asked for an accounting of his property. The first servant had earned ten. The second servant had earned five. The third fellow, living in fear of mak-ing a mistake, had put the thing away in a handkerchief.

Well, the nobleman rewarded the first two and punished the third. But if we read carefully, we see that he rewarded not for the success but for the effort, and he punished not for the lack of success but for the lack of effort.

We can make three general observations from this.

1. It's better to have failed than never to have tried.

Several years ago, I knew two high-school sophomores who were good friends and had many things in common. Each ex-plored the possibility of trying out for the basketball team. They talked at length and dreamed of the success they might enjoy. Finally, one got up the courage and tried out; the other chose not to. Now, to make this a good story, I should tell you that the girl who chose to try out discovered an unlimited hid-den talent, blossomed into greatness, and is now the first woman playing in the NBA. But that story isn't true. In fact, she didn't make the team. Four days after she started, the coach cut her from the squad.

At this point in the story, I personally would rather be the girl who didn't try out. At least she didn't have the humiliation of getting cut. But now, twenty years later, the first woman knows she gave it her best. The second will never know. And I would hate to go through life always wondering what might have happened. Twenty years later, I would rather be the one who tried.

Not long ago, I tried to decide the saddest word in our lan-guage. One nomination was the word *lonely;* that word sounds very sad. But the word I chose as the saddest of all is *almost.*

The second woman has to live her life with that word. I "almost" went out for the basketball team. I "almost" learned to play. I "almost" took that job to see if I could handle it. I "almost" applied to that college. Aren't those sad statements? Yes, it seems to me that "almost" is the stuff of tragedy.

2. It's better to find our limits than never to know our potential.

I was in a locker room the other day, and a sign caught my attention. In typical tough talk, it reminded me, "Losing is worse than death because you have to live with a loss."

What a stupid idea! No wonder locker room wisdom is growing stale. Losing is necessary to find out how good you are. You never know what your potential is until you find the person who can beat you. At that point, you regroup, get better, and try again. That's the stuff of greatness.

I have a friend who is an excellent tennis player, but to keep improving, he has to play people who are better than he is.

The fear of failure, the fear of making mistakes, is the fear of finding your limit; but if you keep underselling yourself, you will never know your potential. As a long-distance road runner, I know I can run five miles. I know I can run ten miles. But can I run a twenty-six-mile marathon? Well, I won't know that until I try. What if I fail and don't make it? Well, at least I've found my limit.

3. It's better to start over than to quit.

That's another joy of mistakes; they teach us when to change directions. But the beautiful thing about life is that we can always start over. Let me mention some of my friends.

• The forty-eight-year-old woman who is graduating from college this spring to enter a teaching career.

• The thirty-two-year-old man who learned to play the bass guitar and has formed a band.

• The thirty-year-old high-school graduate who got fed up with being illiterate and taught himself to read.

• The man who started his acting career at age sixty-five.

• The young man who joined the college football team without ever having played before and wound up being a star.

• The author who wrote seven books before the first was published. Now that book is a best-seller.

The list goes on. These people have one thing in common: They aren't easily discouraged. If they try to make the milk cold and end up with ice cream, they won't stand around and pout about it.

You have a ton of decisions to make just now, and there is a possibility you will make a mistake that could be a major stepping stone in your life.

SCHOOL IS FOR
CHILDREN;
LEARNING IS
FOREVER

It's time to see what you learned in school.

1. You learned that seven times nine is sixty-three when you have time to think about it.

2. You learned that Shakespeare probably wrote all those plays, although most people think he didn't.

3. You learned that George Washington chopped down a cherry tree and told the truth.

4. In science, you learned that a mole is not an animal, although you are still not really clear what it is.

5. In algebra you learned how to factor, but you don't know why or when.

6. In the halls, you learned that a straight line is the shortest distance, but not always the fastest distance, between two points.

7. You learned how to study English during math and not get caught.

8. You learned how to look like you were paying attention when you really weren't.

9. You learned how to take shortcuts when the homework assignment was longer than you had time for.

10. You learned how to learn.

Well, let's at least hope for the last one because that's the goal of a high-school education. It's also the lesson that will be most useful to you both at home and at work.

An old adage says, "It isn't what you know but who you know." I suppose that has a ring of truth to it in certain situations, such as if your father happens to own the company. But I have problems with this comment on life because it sounds so fatalistic. To me, at least when people quote it with a sigh of resignation in their voices, it sounds as if your success depends merely on your connections; and if you don't have the right connections, you may as well forget it, my friend.

Well, I'm not going to buy that, so I offer you a couple of paraphrases.

• It isn't what you know but what you are willing to learn.
• It isn't who you know but who you are willing to meet.

I like these ideas better because they put the responsibility for your success squarely where it belongs—on you.

Let's look at the first point. YOU AREN'T FINISHED LEARNING. I know you don't want to hear that. You've just finished school, turned in the textbooks, burned the notebooks, and forgotten about your grades. You haven't taken a test in a month you don't have another in sight, and you love it. If there is one thing you are tired of, it's learning. But hold on. You can finish school, but you can't finish learning. School is like buying dishes; you can eventually get enough of them. But learning is like keeping them clean, that's an endless endeavor.

Let's hope that you have learned to learn, which is a necessary talent for two reasons.

The world is in transition. If you listen to the people who study such things, they will give you so many statistics that it will make your head spin. In this age of knowledge explosion, information doubles in the time it takes you to wait for a traffic light to change. Most careers of today weren't even dreamed of when people my age were your age. Africa used to be known as the Dark Continent, and it was billions of miles away somewhere. Now it's a short plane ride away.

Most of the time when these people recite all those statistics about the world in transition, we listen with one ear half cocked and go on about our business as usual. But the other day, I caught a short glimpse of the reality of this. Twenty years ago, I spent some time working in a newspaper office. Because it was a small office, I learned many new skills. I talked to the people who were in the profession; I went to classes and workshops; and I learned by trial and error. But I learned, and I was able to do my work.

Last week, for the first time in twenty years, I visited a newspaper office, and I couldn't believe what I saw. Every skill I had worked so hard to master is now obsolete. They don't do those things anymore.

Now, let's take a close look at what this really means. Those people my age who still work in that newspaper office have had to master a completely new set of skills in the past twenty years. They have had to learn. Those who couldn't learn dropped out.

You're in transition. Well, I have said enough about that topic that I won't dwell on it except to remind you that you will always be in something of a transition.

Your ability to adjust to these two realities is found in your willingness to learn.

Not long ago, I read a statement by the president of a giant corporation. He said that American industry must have people who are capable of learning. They don't necessarily need to be trained in a specific field or master a specific skill, but they must be able to learn.

So what is the subject matter of all this learning you have left in front of you? I think you can divide your future learning into three distinct kinds of lessons: the lessons of people, the lessons of places, and the lessons of situations.

The lessons of people. Unless you choose a career as a forest ranger or a lighthouse keeper, you will live the rest of your life in the presence of people. Since every person in this world is distinct and unusual, you will spend the rest of your life learning how to deal with a variety of individuals. That's a thrilling prospect.

You learned some of the necessary skills to survive high school. Shortly after the semester started, you learned what each teacher expected, and you learned what you had to do to meet those expectations. I am sure you learned that, because if you didn't, you wouldn't be graduating.

You will continue to use those skills for the rest of your life. You will work with a variety of people, and frequently, you will find that you must not only do your best but also lead some other person to do his or her best. That is the task of being a parent; of being a spouse; of being a teacher; of being the boss.

The lessons of places. You will probably live in a variety of places in your lifetime. Since each place is distinct and unusual, you will need to master the skill of learning how to survive and thrive in each.

This can be a thrilling prospect, but I know people who have never mastered it. When their responsibilities require them to move to a new place, sometimes right around the corner, they are frustrated and anxious.

The lessons of situations. We could chop this topic up into a thousand little pieces and make it more specific. Some people would want me to tell you that you will have to master new machines, new software programs, new equipment, and new working environments. That's all true, but you master those situations regardless by using the same learning skills.

Let's talk about some of those learning skills that will help you get on top of the lessons of people, places and situations. The educators will call these the skills of problem solving and critical thinking, but because I'm not sure I know what those terms mean, let's break them down even further.

The skill of listening. A great philosopher (I think it was Yogi Berra) once said, "You can sure see a lot just observing." Well, you can sure learn a lot just listening. In fact, of the skills you will learn in your life, the skill of listening will probably be the most valuable of all.

The older I get, the more I realize that almost everybody I meet has something to contribute to my storehouse of knowledge, insight, and problem-solving ability. My job as a learner is to listen.

The skill of asking questions. You have probably heard this before somewhere. I am going to guess that sometime during your high-school career, you had that one rather daring teacher who challenged all of you to ask questions. "Question everything," he would say. "Your right as a human being is to know why." Well, that's all right, but that teacher forgot to tell you something rather significant.

There are two kinds of questions. There are questions you ask out of cynicism. You know the kind. You say to your mom, "Why do I have to be home at 11:30 now that I am a high-school graduate?" And there are questions you ask because you are looking for information and understanding. How does this machine work? Why does it work that way? Why did the Cubans revolt? Who was Adam Bede? What is your job here? Those are the kinds of questions that turn you into a lifelong learner.

The skill of honesty. In high school you learned an important skill called the skill of snow. Let me remind you. One day in English class, you took a test that contained one of those dreaded essay questions. You couldn't even read the question, much less put together a coherent response, but you wrote anyway. And when the paper came back, your answer was worth partial credit.

Now I want to tell you about the opposite skill. It's called the skill of honesty, and it is the skill of a learner. As long as you can bask in the warmth of snow, for partial credit, you will never have to face the fact that you don't know, and you will never become a learner.

There comes a time when snow won't work. Let me give you a for instance.

Someday, you will go to interview for a job. Dressed in your finest with your hair combed and a smile on your face, you will sit across from this interviewer and be scared to death. Surprisingly, you will find yourself doing better than expected, but eventually the dreaded moment will come. The interviewer will ask you a question to which you don't know the answer. What in the world are you going to do? Well, let me tell you what to say at that moment. Just say, "I'm sorry, I don't know." That's what you say when you don't know; you tell the truth. Trying to snow in this situation will only get you in trouble because the interviewer will see you as the phony you are. The skill of honesty is the skill of a learner. In fact, you may want to add this to your speech: "I don't know, but I'm willing to learn." Personally, I find that impressive.

The skill of trial and error. You aren't afraid to make a mistake. You are a learner.

I must confess that I'm offering you this T-shirt for my benefit. I don't know whether its wisdom will ever help you. But I personally like this message, and since I am the one making up the T-shirts, I should be entitled to at least one just for myself.

Actually, I offer the message in self-defense. I like living in this world, and I would like to see this world go on for a while until Jesus decides to come again.

However, you must realize that you are living in a world of interesting possibilities. Of course, I am not smart enough to think of these on my own, but the scholars talk about the possibility to leave the earth and the possibility to destroy it.

Both are rather new uncertainties. Your generation is the first to graduate from high school and face the possible reality of either or both. For that reason, I want to talk about revolutions.

As you know, progress doesn't always move in a straight line creeping upward. Sometimes progress comes in little starts and stops that tend to bump into each other. Sometimes those little starts and stops are the results of revolutions.

You remember studying about them. You studied the French Revolution, the American Revolution, the Russian Revolution, and lots of others.

As you studied, you realized that revolutions come when people get sick and tired of the old ways and refuse to put up with them anymore. The people in power get worse until the situation is unbearable; then the people being pushed around join forces, and revolt, and win. The old power is dethroned, beheaded, drawn and quartered, or shot. The old ways end never to return.

But that's just the problem. The revolution is only half over. The world never lives in a vacuum. When we destroy the old ways, new ways rise up to take their place, and these new ways have to come from somewhere.

Let's look at how this worked out in history. During the French Revolution, the people got rid of the king named Louis, but Napoleon Bonaparte rose up to take his place. That wasn't much of a bargain.

The Russians got rid of the czars, but the Bolsheviks rose up to take their place. That wasn't much of a bargain. The Cubans got rid of Batista, but Castro rose up to take his place. That wasn't much of a bargain.

Are you getting the picture? Putting down the old is only half the battle; that's why most revolutions fail. The revolutionaries, for all their good intentions, are only half-prepared. They know what they want to destroy. But too often they don't know what will replace it, and they don't know how to move to where they want to be.

"Sure," you say, "that's a good history lesson. But what does it have to do with me? You always talk about something that happened hundreds of years ago that doesn't have any practical value in my life."

But this lesson does. In one way or another, you will always be involved in some kind of revolution. Who knows? You may get involved in some great worldwide movement, or you may just be making some personal decision. But in either situation, you will be involved in a revolution.

Let me illustrate. Often someone your age says to me, "I've got to quit this job. Do you have any idea of what I'm going through?" And then I hear an endless recitation of all the injustices and cruelties of the old job—things like:

"I have to work overtime."

"I never get to work overtime."

"I get too much supervision."

"I don't get enough supervision."

"My boss hates me."

"My boss loves me and bores me."

"I don't get enough money."

"I get too much money." Whoops, I got carried away with these contrasts. I have *never* heard that last one.

Nevertheless, the person has convinced himself that he must quit. He must get rid of the old ways. He knows what he wants to be rid of.

The next question is so obvious that you would think it could never be overlooked, but it almost always is. "If you quit your old job, what will you get for a new job?" It is so obvious and so logical that we often forget it completely, but we run into this kind of one-way revolution all the time.

"I need to get rid of this present husband (or wife)."

"I need to get rid of this old car."

"We need to get rid of this old house."

"We need to fire our minister."

"We need to vote this man out of office."

"I need to quit this school."

About the time you catch yourself saying something like

this, you need to stop and remember that this is only half the revolution. If this is as far as you have planned, you are only half-prepared and that isn't enough.

If you need a reminder, just glance down at your T-shirt.

LOVE IS AN ACT
OF OBEDIENCE

Is there an end to all these T-shirts?" you ask. "I have a drawerful now."

But the other question is, "Is there an end to all the changes hitting me in the face?"

This particular shirt is a forceful reminder of the changes in your life during this time of transition.

Regardless of what you do now or in the next four years, regardless of where you live, where you work, or what you learn, you are going to experience some changes in your relationships. You are going to pick up some new friends and change the way you relate to the old ones. You may not pick up any new parents, but you will definitely change the way you relate to the old ones. You definitely won't pick up a new

God—there's only one of those—but you will probably change the way you relate to Him.

And that's what this T-shirt is about; it's an introduction to the topic of relationships. It announces to the world, and reminds you of, the basic ingredient of relationships—love.

What a big assignment we have given to such a little word. No wonder it sounds overworked at times. In one day, by myself, I've said:

"I love cherry pie."

"I love Friday evenings when there is no school tomorrow."

"I love jokes that don't offend anyone."

"I love harmonica music."

"I love this country."

"I love my wife."

"I love Jesus Christ."

Every statement is accurate enough, but not in the same way. Obviously, I don't feel the same way toward cherry pie as I feel toward my wife. And as patriotic as I am, I don't feel the same way toward my country as I feel toward my Savior.

What we have here is a breakdown in communication. We have that one little word doing too much work. It needs some help, so I've come to the rescue.

We definitely need some new words to express ourselves without saying "love" all the time. These new words need to sound like English; but they need to be new words, not old ones with new jobs. Thus, add these following entries to that new dictionary you got for a graduation gift.

grunch *vt:* The active feeling that two members of the opposite sex carry for each other which is half the distance between friendship and matrimony. For example, when a boy takes a girl home following an enjoyable time out where he has spent tons of money on food and entertainment and they stand together in the moonlight at her doorstep, it would be appropriate for her to look into his eyes and say with conviction, "I grunch you."

gewalzit *vt:* The showing of intense pride that one has for his country. For example, I gewalzit America and always will.

What do you think? Do these have promise or what? Well, maybe you're right. Maybe love sounds better after all. So let's see if we can come up with an operational definition of love so that the old word will communicate for us.

Try this: Love is the commitment that carries the relationship through the storms.

"Wait a minute," you protest. "I don't like the idea of storms. Why start negatively? If I really love somebody, there won't be any storms. Isn't that the whole idea of friends in the first place?"

Well, not really. It's nice to start positively, but we do need to be wise. Jesus talked about being wise and told a little story about two house builders. He called one wise and the other foolish. (See Matt. 7:24–27.)

Do you remember the difference between them? The foolish builder forgot about the storms. He built his house right on the sand, and the storms did it in. On the other hand, the wise man built his house on a rock, and his house withstood the storms.

That's the analogy of love. It's the foundation that carries the relationship through the storms.

In all probability, there will be a few storms in your friendships. But there is something stronger than the storms.

There could be storms in your relationship with your parents. But there is something stronger than the storms.

There may be a storm in your marriage someday. But there is something stronger than the storm.

There could even be a storm in your relationship with God. But there is something stronger than the storm.

That's the reassuring promise of love. It will carry us through.

Of course, now that we have a definition of love, we need to decide how to master it. That may be the tough part.

I think that as an old-timer I should have the privilege of giving you upstarts a lecture about how the modern age has ruined the old-fashioned notion of love with ideas of infatuation and physical attraction. I think I am supposed to blame all that on Hollywood. You know how it sounds. "Well, that Hollywood idea of love will corrupt us for sure."

But Hollywood was not the first culprit. Even in Shakespeare's plays you find people running around the forest at night throwing goofy dust on people and making them fall in love with donkeys and all sorts of things. So let's blame it on Shakespeare.

Can you see the old-timers in the seventeenth century sitting around complaining about those new notions of love people were picking up down at the Globe Theater?

Regardless of who's to blame, we still have the idea that love is something mystical—something beyond comprehension. "I don't know how it happened. We were just going out together and bang—one night we just fell in love." Well, I won't argue with that, but I have trouble with the other side of that coin.

"I don't know how it happened. They have been my parents for eighteen years, but bang—one night I stopped loving them."

No—love isn't something we fall in and out of on a whim. Love is the commitment that endures.

The Bible tells me to love my wife. There isn't any hint of magical potions and powders. I am to love my wife as an act of obedience to God.

The other day, I watched a crane driving pillars into the ground for the foundation of a high-rise building. The crane was a massive machine with gigantic tires, a tall boom way up above everything, and a huge ball that served as a battering ram driving those pillars. The operator sitting in the cab was so far away and so tiny in comparison that he seemed insignificant to the whole operation.

I was struck by the force of the machine, by the power inherent in each blow of the ball; and I wondered, "Is this machine the greatest constructive force in all the world?"

Of course it isn't. Love is the most powerful constructive force in all the world. Because of love, Jesus came to earth. Because of love, my wife greets me every day; my mother calls me; my grown children ask my advice; and my friends visit me.

The powerful life, the one worth living, is the one filled with love. To reach toward that power, we need to learn to give love and to receive love. We need to hear the word of the Lord, and do it. Love is simply obeying God.

THE WORLD GOES
AROUND ON ITS
OWN—BUT
FRIENDS
GREASE THE AXLE

An old adage says that to have a friend, you have to be one.

Emerson once wrote that a friend is a person with whom you can think aloud.

Mark Twain once remarked, "It takes two people to hurt you—your enemy to criticize you and your friend to get the news to you."

You know the truth of all these comments because you have been actively involved in friendships; those friendships have played a significant role in your development.

Your parents were scared to death when you started junior high because they were worried about the friends you would make. As all parents know, a monster called peer pressure lurks in the halls of every junior high, just waiting to ruin children.

Do you remember how you sometimes acted strange back then in the name of friendship? Do you remember the time that you and your friends decided to spend the evening at the mall, but your mother refused to take you because of some silly reason like a snowstorm? You would have done almost anything to get to your friends.

Do you remember the time you bought a Miss Piggy notebook because that's what all your friends had?

Do you remember the time your best friend liked somebody better than you, and it ruined your whole day?

Do you remember that all-night graduation party when you met all your buddies and promised to be the best of friends forever? Yet in a short while you realized that you hadn't seen those people and hadn't really missed them all that much. What's going on here?

In the midst of all the other changes that accompany high-school graduation, maybe friendships and friendship patterns undergo some changes as well. It is a definite possibility.

I would venture a rather bold guess that the friends you had four years ago when you started high school weren't the friends you had at the end. Of course, you might have maintained a relationship with one best friend or maybe even a little clique of three or four. But for the most part, you just don't have the same friends. Your friends have changed, and your friendship patterns have changed some, too.

I am going to venture a guess that the friends you had on graduation night won't be the same friends you will have four years from now. But that isn't really as frightening as it sounds. Making friends is an exciting enterprise, and it is one of the joys of life itself.

It probably is appropriate at this time that we ponder some virtues of friendships. That way you know what is happening to you, and you might even take charge of the process. I once heard a man say that the changes in our lives are the results of the books we read and the people we meet. For that reason alone, the concept of friendship deserves some thought.

1. Friendships are the most rewarding form of entertainment. I put this one first because it smacks of fun, and fun is definitely a part of friendship. We make friends with people because we enjoy being with them. We go with our friends to movies or basketball games, but when it is all over, we realize that the best part was the friendship and not the activity. Joy, fun, and good times are the outgrowths of our friendships.

2. Friendships lift us out of loneliness. Now that you are out of high school you may not be around lots of people every day, and you may discover something about the pains of loneliness. The only way to combat loneliness is to have a friend. It's important that you remember this now, as you and your past friends begin to move in separate directions.

3. Friendships help us identify our moods. How often have you noticed that your friend's mood becomes your mood? It's a rather typical response. I have friends who make me happy and positive about myself and the world. On the other hand, I have friends who set a certain ring of pessimism into everything, and they make me feel cranky and depressed. In recent years, I have learned enough about myself to try to stay around that first group. Now I'm beginning to wonder what kind of friend I am.

4. Friendships help us remember our experiences. Regardless of what we do or where we do it, life is full. There is much to see, hear, taste, and smell. If you have a friend who will listen to you, you can relate some of these impressions, and they become a part of your storehouse of pleasant memories. On the other hand, if you don't have a friend, you have to rely on your own good memory.

Do you remember when you went on your first date? You later met your friend and gave a blow-by-blow account. Some might accuse you of being the kind that kiss and tell, but I see it another way. It was just a way you had of verbalizing the experience so that it became a part of your memory. You will need friends for this reason for the rest of your life.

5. Friendships become our schools. Now that the classes are over, the lectures are finished, and the tests have been scored, you will learn most of your lessons from your friends.

Now that we have discussed the values of friendships, it might seem that we should spend some time talking about how to form friendships. But that discussion is probably not necessary. You have made friends before; you will make friends again by using the same techniques.

It might also seem necessary for us to talk about friendships with the opposite sex, but we are not going to do that, either. Lots of books about dating are available. Again, you know all the techniques. At this point, it is just necessary for you to realize that in this time of transition, dating takes on a new set of rules, too.

No, at this point, it should be sufficient for you to realize that your friends and friendship patterns will change. There is no need to panic—just take charge.

IF I DON'T LAUGH
AT ME,
EVERYBODY
ELSE WILL

Everyone sings the praises of laughter.

Some people call it a miracle healing drug. The *Reader's Digest* calls it the best medicine. A sign in a classroom reminded me, "A laugh a day keeps the doctor away." So just to stay healthy, I laughed. The teacher scowled, and I left the room.

A few years ago, a well-known journalist developed a very serious disease, and he healed himself with laughter. (Well, at least that is what he said. Maybe something else healed him, but he just wanted an excuse to watch old Three Stooges movies.)

You probably know something about the healing virtue of laughter. Do you remember the time you weren't feeling well but you went to the party anyway and soon forgot that you were sick?

Some people tell us that laughter is valuable to learning. Of course, if you get carried away with that in class, it could be dangerous. Did you ever have that teacher who tried to tell jokes but shouldn't have? But perhaps just his trying to be funny was funny anyway.

Some people tell us that laughter is valuable for easing tension and calming nerves. You probably know something about that, too. Do you remember the time you were in a meeting and things got tense? Then someone cracked a joke, and order was restored.

Of course, laughter is a valuable tool for getting through life. But you knew that already. You really don't need a T-shirt to remind you of that point.

What we are never really quite clear about is where laughter comes from. If you ask the average person in the street, you will probably get some answer from the world of entertainment.

"Tell me, sir, where does laughter come from?"

"Jay Leno," he is likely to say, or "David Letterman," or maybe "Milton Berle" if the person is ancient.

But somehow, we know that's not the answer. After all, some nights you watch Jay Leno and don't laugh at all. That's because laughter has to come from within ourselves. As a matter of fact, laughter is the result of the way we look at ourselves.

Regardless of how funny the joke is, laughter is still a very personal and private approach to life. That's the lesson of this shirt. When we laugh at others, that is cruel. But when we laugh at ourselves, that is joy. The ability to laugh at ourselves is the first characteristic of a happy life. If you don't have it, you won't have much happiness.

In short, never take yourself too seriously. Now this isn't a lesson that we learn once and know for the rest of our lives. It is something we have to learn over and over again. That's why we need the T-shirt. I could stop here and tell you a thousand personal stories that illustrate the value of laughter in my life. But you have stories of your own—stories that constantly remind you that there really is humor in life if we can just take the time to stop and look inside.

NOW THAT I'VE GROWN UP, MY PARENTS ARE GETTING SMARTER

You graduate; you get a job; you change your friends; and your parents grow up. It's a strange world, the world of transitions.

Regardless of all that is changing in your life right now, your relationship with your parents is about to undergo a major transition, too. Oh, it may be subtle. You may not sense any real difference in the way you feel about them or in the way they seem to feel about you, but the relationship is going to change, anyway.

For one thing, you are going to achieve a little more freedom in the relationship. It may be something as subtle as your curfew being lifted. I know this sounds minor, but it indicates bigger and more profound changes in the way you and your parents look at each other.

On the other hand, the change may be as drastic as your moving out of your parents' house completely. If that's the case, you're probably completely excited about it. You've now achieved one of the major goals in life—you're not living at home anymore.

But reread what I just said: "Not living at home anymore." I said it that way on purpose to trick you. If you associate the word *home* with that place where you and your parents lived, leaving it is going to be a significant emotional event. You need to prepare for it a bit.

How are you going to feel, knowing that life still goes on in that place but you are not a part of it? How are you going to feel when your parents turn your bedroom into a sewing room; when you go to the bathroom you used for eighteen years and discover that your toothbrush isn't hanging there anymore; when you go for a drink of water only to discover someone rearranged the dishes, and you can't find the glasses?

You'll probably be a bit distraught about this drastic change in your life. I am not harping on this to send you into despair. I just want to remind you that your relationship with your parents is going to change, and I want to warn you about some of the traps I've seen people your age fall into.

When you first leave home, you will probably spend some time feeling sorry for yourself. Oh, sure, you can tell me about this freedom bit and all the things you plan to do with it. But you don't fool anybody—you are going to be homesick. It may be such a light case that you get a little twinge of loneliness once in a while, or it may be a severe case where you cry yourself to sleep for weeks on end. Either way, the homesickness tells you that your relationship with your parents is changing.

Some people try to fight the homesickness by rejecting their parents. They decide, subconsciously, that the way to handle this problem is to lose contact with home. In other words, they shut their parents out of their lives. They don't write; they don't call; they don't take orders from home anymore.

Some people turn their backs on the lessons their parents instilled through the years. They rebel against the authority of their parents and do things that they know their parents would disapprove of. To them, freedom means breaking away from parental influence altogether. That tells me that the relationship has definitely changed.

The process of leaving home is exciting, but it does come with all sorts of strange emotions, frustrations, and anxieties. You'll experience some bumps and bruises along the way. Again, I warn you about these because in your eagerness to become independent you may not spend enough time planning for some richly needed security.

At that time when your relationship with your parents is undergoing significant overhaul and redevelopment, I recommend that you attempt to find some needed understanding and security from your parents themselves. Isn't that a strange paradox?

But of all the people who could understand you and what you are going through, your parents are probably first on the list. You may get the idea that your parents' only intention is to cramp your style and limit your vision. In short, you may feel that they don't understand you at all and want only to cramp your style and limit your vision.

But that's probably not true. Your parents understand you in a way that goes beyond common sense, logic, and best advice. They understand you with love, and that's the greatest understanding of all.

That's why I make my recommendation. Love is such a priceless commodity that we really shouldn't turn our backs on it when it's offered to us. Although your relationship with your parents is changing, it isn't a sign of weakness for you to maintain an open, honest, communicative relationship with them.

If you will work at keeping the love relationship alive, in a few years you will discover something amazing. You'll be an adult, and you'll notice that your parents have become smarter. It is a strange phenomenon, but it almost always works that way. Somehow, the parents of adults are always smarter and better informed than the parents of adolescents. In fact, you may even discover that your parents are among the smartest people you know. But why shouldn't it work this way? Did you think you were the only one changing during all this time?

GOD IS SMARTER
THAN I AM

When you wear this message, the people you meet will think, *Well, that's obvious.* You may even catch them snickering a bit that you would label your chest with such an obvious point.

In fact, don't be surprised if some stop you and tell you a story to document the obvious. The intellectuals who stop you will even have a big name for this. They will describe God as being sovereign.

I don't know what sovereign means, but I have been learning the lesson that God is smarter than I am. As I go through life, I realize every moment of every day that God is smarter than I am.

For all of my efforts to make plans, carry them out, analyze my talents, and take charge of my life, I am still reminded every minute of every day that God is smarter than I am.

When I got married, I thought I had taken charge of the process since I had chosen my wife. But now, more than three decades later, I realize that I could never have been smart enough to make that choice work out the way it has. Surely, God was supervising.

I also thought I took charge of choosing my career. But now I realize that I could never have been smart enough to have made the choice work out the way it has. Surely, God was supervising.

Once during my career, I moved to a new place, and I had a hard time adjusting to the change. I was unhappy, and I wondered what had happened to God's intervention in my life. But now, in my present position, I call on the experiences I had in that place at least once a week. I could never have been smart enough to know that those experiences would be so valuable to me now. Surely, God was supervising.

I offer you my personal experiences for assurance. If you're like most new graduates, you are probably scared to death. You know in vivid terms that you are facing a period of adjustment. You know that you are making significant decisions about your future, and you are sweating out every one. It's enough to make you want to jump into bed, pull the covers up, and stay there for the next twenty years.

But I give you a message of hope—God is smarter than you are. As you make the decisions and ponder the future, keep in mind that God is at work in your life.

Maybe that's what sovereignty means—the promise of life and the assurance that makes it all enjoyable.